KEEPING YOUR KIDS CHRISTIAN

Keeping Your Kids Christian

*A Candid Look at One of
the Greatest Challenges Parents Face*

Edited by
Marshall Shelley

Servant Publications
Ann Arbor, Michigan

Vine Books is an imprint of Servant Publications especially
designed to serve Evangelical Christians.

Published by Servant Publications
P.O. Box 8617
Ann Arbor, Michigan 48107

Cover design by Michael Andaloro
Cover illustration by Gerry Gawronski

90 91 92 93 94   10 9 8 7 6 5 4 3 2 1

Printed in the United States of America
ISBN 0-89283-667-9

Library of Congress Cataloging-in-Publication Data

Keeping your kids Christian : a candid look at one of the
    greatest challenges parents face. / edited by Marshall
Shelley.
        p.   cm.
    ISBN 0-89283-667-9
    1. Family—Religious life.   2. Parenting—Religious aspects—
Christianity.   3. Youth—Religious life.   I. Shelley, Marshall.
BV4526.2.K43   1990
248.8'45—dc20   90-37963
                                                      CIP

Contents

Contributors

Stephen Arterburn is founder and chairman of New Life Treatment Centers, Inc., a company treating people with drug and alcohol problems, eating disorders, and compulsive sexual behavior. He coauthored with Jim Burns the book *Drug-Proof Your Kids*. He and his wife, Sandy, live in Laguna Beach, California.

V. Gilbert Beers is considered a foremost authority on Christian literature for children, with six million copies of his children's books in print, including *The Children's Illustrated Bible Dictionary*. A former editor of *Christianity Today*, Gil and his wife, Arlie, live in Elgin, Illinois, where they raised five children.

Joy Bolin is a mother of three and grandmother of seven. She leads seminars on marriage and motherhood, and she's involved with a counseling program for dependents and co-dependents of alcohol and drug abuse. Her husband, Tom, is minister of administration and programs at First Baptist Church, Katy, Texas.

D. Ross Campbell, M.D., is a psychiatrist and founder of Southeastern Counseling Center in Chattanooga, Tennessee, where he is in private practice. He is the author of such books as *How to Really Love Your Child* and *How to Really Love Your Teenager*. He and his wife Pat raised four children.

James Dobson is the head of Focus on the Family, an organization dedicated to strengthening family life, headquartered in Pomona, California. He has written numerous books, including *Dare to Discipline, Hide and Seek,* and *Love Must Be Tough.* He and his wife, Shirley, have two children.

Richard R. and **Teresa Dunn** live in Wildwood, Illinois, where Richard teaches and serves as chairman of the youth ministry department at Trinity College in Deerfield, Illinois.

Gloria Gaither and her husband, Bill, are writers, arrangers, and performers of Christian music, living in Alexandria, Indiana. Gloria, along with Shirley Dobson, wrote the book *Let's Make a Memory.* The Gaithers have three children.

Eddy Hall is a free-lance writer and editor. His work has appeared in such publications as *Leadership* and *The Christian Leader.* He and his wife, Melody, live in Goessel, Kansas with their four children.

Jay Kesler is president of Taylor University in Upland, Indiana. He was previously president of Youth for Christ/ USA. He has numerous books to his credit, including *Parents and Teens,* and a radio program titled "Family Forum." He and his wife, Janie, have raised three children.

Jean Lush, coauthor of the best-selling *Mothers and Sons,* is a frequent guest on James Dobson's "Focus on the Family" radio program. She is a therapist on the staff of the Crista Counseling Service in Edmonds, Washington.

Gordon MacDonald is pastor of Trinity Baptist Church in New York City. He is the author of several books, including *Ordering Your Private World* and *The Effective Father.* He and his wife, Gail, have raised two children.

Louis McBurney, M.D. and his wife **Melissa** have cofounded Marble Retreat, a counseling center for clergy and their spouses, located in Marble, Colorado. Louis, a psychiatrist, and Melissa have raised three children.

Kevin Miller is editor of *Christian History* magazine and contributing editor of *Marriage Partnership* magazine. He is the author of *Secrets of Staying Power*. He and his wife, Karen, live in Glendale Heights, Illinois, and have two children.

Luis and **Pat Palau** live in Portland, Oregon, and have four sons. Luis has spoken in person to more than eight million people in fifty nations in his role as head of The Luis Palau Evangelistic Team, which sponsors evangelistic crusades, leadership training, and media programs. His wife, Pat, has an active conference ministry.

Marshall Shelley is editor of *Leadership,* a journal for church leaders. He is the author of *Well-Intentioned Dragons, The Healthy Hectic Home,* and *Telling Stories to Children*. He and his wife, Susan, live in Wheaton, Illinois, with their three daughters.

Carol Smith is associate editor of preschool products at Scripture Press in Wheaton, Illinois. A graduate of Bryan College in Tennessee and Southwestern Theological Seminary in Texas, she served four years as minister of childhood education in a Fort Worth church.

Tim Stafford is a contributing editor to *Christianity Today* and a columnist answering teenagers' questions about "Love, Sex, and the Whole Person" in *Campus Life* magazine. He and his wife, Popie, live in Santa Rosa, California, with their three children.

Barbara A. Stevenson is executive director of Crisis Pregnancy Center in Charlotte, North Carolina. She is a speaker at women's conferences and Bible classes. Her husband, Glenn, is minister of education at Charlotte's Northside Baptist Church. She and Glenn have raised three children.

Roger Thompson is pastor of Trinity Baptist Church in

Wheat Ridge, Colorado. Previously he served as a copastor at Bear Valley Baptist Church in Denver. He and his wife, Joanne, are raising two daughters.

John Trent is vice president of Today's Family, which has sponsored marriage and family conferences in cities across the United States and Canada. Along with Gary Smalley, he has written *The Blessing, The Gift of Honor, The Language of Love*, and *Love Is a Decision*. He and his wife, Cynthia Ann, live in Phoenix, Arizona and have two children.

Pamela Vredevelt is a family counselor in Gresham, Oregon, and coauthor of several books. Among them are *Surviving the Secret, Women Who Compete,* and *Mothers and Sons.*

Craig and **Carolyn Williford** are raising two sons. Craig is minister of education at South Park Church in Park Ridge, Illinois. Carolyn is a homemaker and author who published *Devotions for Families that Can't Sit Still.*

John W. Yates III is rector of Falls Church (Episcopal) in Falls Church, Virginia. **Susan Yates** is author of *And Then I Had Kids: Encouragement for Mothers of Young Children.* Together John and Susan speak at family conferences and are raising five children.

Introduction

AN AUTHOR DEDICATED ONE OF HIS BOOKS: "To my two sons, teachers in the art of family living, who in the process have put gray hairs on my head, bills in my pocket, ideas in my books, happiness in my home, and pride in my heart."

This writer captures some of the mixed emotions parents feel about raising kids: it's a tough job, you never feel adequately prepared, things happen unpredictably, and you learn that worry and disappointment usually come intermingled with satisfaction and joy.

Those of us who are Christian parents have an additional concern. We want our children to grow up to love God and live for him. We can't make our children's decisions for them, but we can make sure that the atmosphere of our home is conducive to growing in faith and that our children learn about the love God offers us in Christ. How they respond, of course, is not within our control.

A friend of mine, Scott Bolinder, helped me understand this slippery aspect of parenting. His daughter Anna, age four-and-a-half, was still attached to a tattered, ripped "security blanket."

One day Anna announced to her parents that she was going to throw out her blanket. Scott was convinced she didn't understand the gravity of her seemingly impetuous decision. He reviewed the consequences.

"Once you throw your blanket out, Anna, it's gone. You won't be able to get it back. Understand?"

"I know," she said simply.

Scott took her to the curb where the garbage cans stood, looked her in the eye, and said, "Well, if you are really ready to throw your blankie out, then *you* put it in the garbage." (Scott said later, "I wasn't going to be the bad guy, guilty of throwing away her security.")

Anna decisively placed the blanket in the trash.

"We never heard another word about the blanket," Scott recalls. "But that night, my wife, Jill, and I both remarked how difficult it was for *us* to see Anna take this developmental stride. For us, it marked the end of an era. What should have been a cause for great celebration (finally, she's getting rid of that crummy thing and growing up!) left us strangely melancholy. We felt like our kids were growing up too fast, and before we knew it, they'd be gone."

Reflecting, Scott said: "They say a parent's job is to give his kids two things—one is roots, the other is wings."

Roots are the experiences and nurture parents provide that allow a child to grow strong enough to live in this world. Wings are the progressively greater freedoms we grant children to allow them to mature.

This book is about both roots and wings—giving children firm roots in the essentials of the Christian faith, but also helping them develop their wings, so they can make the faith their own and make their own mark on the world.

Three elements are at work in providing the roots of the faith: knowing, doing, and being.

Rootedness starts with knowing. Psalm 100:3 says, "*Know* that the Lord is God. It is he who made us, and we are his; we are his people, the sheep of his pasture." In Ephesians 1:18, Paul prays that the people "may *know* the hope to which he has called you, the riches of his glorious inheritance."

As we will see in this book, there are many ways parents can make sure children are rooted in the right knowledge. But knowing, while essential, is not enough. This knowledge requires action. In the Old Testament, God tells his people repeatedly, "observe to do." In the New Testament,

Jesus makes clear that hearing must be accompanied by doing. Or, as James says, "I will show you my faith by what I do" (Jas 2:18).

Finally, Christian maturity is more than knowing and doing. It's being. That means faith becomes a personal trait, something that characterizes an individual. The fruit of the Spirit—love, joy, peace, patience, kindness, gentleness—are not so much things you *do* as things you *are.* This is where roots give way to wings.

This book offers practical help to parents who want their children to learn the content, practice the virtues, and develop the values of a living Christian faith.

And to parents who struggle with children who aren't doing these things, the book offers help in remaining faithful parents, even when a child's response is not encouraging. As Puritan preacher Jonathan Edwards once said, "Resolved: that everyone should live for the glory of God. Resolved second: that whether others do or not, I will."

We mustn't underestimate the power of parents, however, to shape the values and decisions of their children. For example, Randy Pope, who grew up as the son of a dentist, reflects on his father's influence on his values:

"When I was growing up, my father was a dentist. And dentistry, I learned later, is one of the professions with the highest rates of suicide. I don't know all the reasons why, but I can imagine some: you have to take out large loans to get started, you're forced to do precise work in a very confined area (a mouth), you inflict pain and discomfort, people dread seeing you, you're rarely paid promptly.

"But I never heard my dad say anything negative about his profession. I only heard him talk about the benefits: 'Isn't it great that I don't get called in the middle of the night like surgeons do?' 'I'm sure thankful people don't die from dental problems.' 'Dentistry is a great way to help people.' 'I'm really fortunate to be a dentist.'

"As a result of my dad's outlook, there was time in my

adolescence when I wanted to be a dentist, not because I knew anything about it, but because my dad had convinced me it was a privilege."

Randy Pope did not become a dentist, however. He's a pastor—at Perimeter Church in Atlanta. But he's trying to do for his children what his father did for him—to show them that the work he does, the Christian faith he lives, is not a problem but a privilege.

It is to this end—instilling in our children a love and life-changing appreciation for Jesus Christ—that this book is written.

—Marshall Shelley
Wheaton, Illinois
January, 1990

Part 1

The Parent's Role

ONE

What Do You Want Your Children to Become?

V. Gilbert Beers

REMEMBER THE WELL-MEANING MAN who patted you on the head when you were a little boy or girl and asked, "What do you want to be when you grow up?" That's a nervous question, usually asked when an adult doesn't know what else to say.

You know the standard answers. Boys will say fireman, policeman, pilot, or big-league athlete. Girls might answer with nurse, stewardess, or movie star. To a child these are visible people who make things happen. Usually a child thinks of the visibility, such as the uniform, with no conception of the work itself.

Unfortunately, many parents carry similar stereotypes concerning their child's future occupation. Many fathers who dreamed of being a professional ball player push their sons into Little Leagues with a hidden purpose—to live vicariously through the boys.

AUTHENTIC CHRISTIAN GOALS

Have you ever asked yourself what you *really* want your child to be when he or she grows up? Please don't think of a profession or vocation when you ask. That's for your child to decide later on. I think we parents do untold damage if we try to push our children toward any specific job without truly knowing if the child is going to be effective and happy in that job. Let's get out of the business of trying to nudge our children into specific vocations, even vocations that are ministry or missionary oriented. Give God and your child the freedom to work together on those matters.

Yet, as Christian parents there are certain specific goals we should desire for our children as they grow. And we should work with all our energy to make these goals attainable by our children. It's part of the God-given responsibility of being a Christian parent.

Let me share some of the goals that Arlie and I have desired for our children (and grandchildren). We have invested our lives to see these goals accomplished, and we believe that is happening. Perhaps you want these same goals for your children. Or you may have some others.

1. *As early as possible, I want my children to come to know God through Christ, to accept Jesus as their own personal Savior.*

2. *I want them to learn to practice the presence of the living God each day.* I want them to grow daily to be more Christlike, more godly.

3. *I want them to grow to love God's Word* and develop habits of daily Bible reading, not merely because they *should* read it, but because they *desire* to read it.

4. *I want them to cultivate an effective prayer life,* and a life of sharing their faith with others, again, not because they *should* do these things but because they truly *desire* to do them.

5. *I want my children to learn to live by biblical values,* such as honesty, faithfulness, truthfulness, generosity, love, patience, obedience, friendliness, self-control, self-confidence,

courage, compassion, loyalty, thankfulness, perseverance, and helpfulness. I want them to learn to incorporate these values into their daily decisions and daily conduct. Whatever they do in their life at home, in business, in the professions, or in government should be tempered by these values.

6. *I want my children to be men and women of God.* I want them to understand what discipleship means, to follow God obediently even when the cost is high.

7. *I want them to be exemplary role models as Christians* so that other people will desire God because they see God at work winsomely in my children's lives. Their Christian conduct is not to be something stern and demeaning but something beautiful, fragrant, and uplifting. When others watch their conduct they are attracted to Christ, not frightened into his presence.

8. *I want my children to be effective in their chosen work.* I do not intend to choose that work for any one of them, or even subtly campaign for my preferences. But I do hope they will do their best at whatever work they choose. And I do expect them to stay away from vocations that would not bring honor to God.

9. *I want my children to put their mates and their children at the highest order of priority in their lives.* I've learned that family is basic, and that happiness depends on getting family in the rightful place of priority ahead of other things. I hope my children put no one but God above their family.

10. *I want my children to adopt God's priorities for service.* If they choose to live in modest circumstances to serve God in a certain way, that is a noble choice which I would applaud. If they choose to serve God under uncomfortable circumstances, I will pray with them for God's grace to endure. If they choose service that is not a "Christian vocation," but

still have a heart to serve God, I will consider them God's servants.

11. *I want my children to keep earning and spending and giving money in proper perspective.* I pray that they will never be consumed with earning so much that they will neglect God or their family. I want them to keep the pursuit and the careful management of resources in balance. I pray that they will never be consumed with the desire to be wealthy for the sake of wealth, but only be consumed with the desire to gratefully manage their wealth for God in a way that will please him.

12. *I want my children to be disciplined people.* I want them to understand that, like monetary resources, their lives are a trust from God, to be managed carefully for the greatest good and the greatest effectiveness.

13. *I want my children to enter into the delights of life with enthusiasm.* I want them to appreciate their work, to be grateful for the scent of a rose or the taste of pancakes on a winter morning. I want them to delight in taking their children out in the forest to appreciate the leaves and wildflowers, the birds and woodland creatures, to gaze in awe at the clouds in the sky, to be delighted with the sunset and the harvest moon rising in the autumn sky. I want my children to enthusiastically impart to their children an affinity with the Creator through the enjoyment of his footprints and fingerprints.

14. *I want my children to look at life with a proper mixture of seriousness and good humor.* There is a time to walk into God's presence with a hush. There is a time to laugh uproariously—yes, even laugh at ourselves and our strange ways. I believe that God has a sense of humor, and I hope my children will also maintain a sense of humor.

15. *I want my children to be redemptive with their lives.* That is, I want them to be *life-changers*. When they do something I

hope they will do it for God, or for another person, but not primarily for self. Self-preservation pursued at all costs will cause self-destruction. Our very growth as Christians requires that we invest our lives redemptively for God and others.

16. *In their work, I want my children to be servant leaders.* As Christ came to serve, so they and I as Christians are called to be Christlike. That requires us to serve as he served.

MAKING IT HAPPEN

Having listed all of these wonderful things that I want my children (and grandchildren) to become, how do I help them reach these objectives, assuming that they too want to reach them?

I could outline these objectives for my children and tell them that this is what I want, and perhaps make a manual and go over it daily, or hang this list over the doorway of their room. I could nag them daily to fulfill my expectations. But you who are parents know that these tactics, if they have any effect, will probably reverse the children's progress toward goals such as these.

How can we ask children to become kind and loving and patient, for example, if we try to force them to be kind and loving and patient? I have seen parents try this approach, and it backfires, turning child against parent. You cannot force anyone to love something! You cannot force anyone to desire something, except that you would get off his back!

There is another way. I could outline these objectives for my children and beg them daily for my sake and theirs, and even for God's sake, to do these things. Perhaps I could even shed a few tears. But you parents also know that this will not work. You simply cannot lead children to be kind, loving, and patient by making them feel guilty or making them feel that they are doing it to please you. No, that will not work much better than trying to force them to be kind, loving, and patient.

There is a better way than nagging, pressuring, or applying guilt to create character in our children. As parents, we may role-model our goals for them, living out these goals in our own lives. If these goals are important for your children, you will stress their importance by making them your own goals. Your children will want to be like you when you model these goals, because they will see that you truly believe in them and are trying to make them happen in your own life. Our lives as role models become testimonials rather than commandments. "Don't do as I do, do as I say" will send your children down the road in the opposite direction.

When we live out our goals ourselves first, we gravitate naturally to daily conversations that allow us to share with our children what is important to us. If they see that we are not living what we are saying, they will think we are mocking them. (Perhaps we are!) If they see that we are living what we are saying, they will listen.

On a radio interview one day a thoughtless mother said to me that she had two-hour devotionals with her children each day. I asked how they kept quiet that long. She said she had a big wooden spoon and when they lost attention she would whack them with it. That poor deluded mother will wonder someday why her children turn against Christianity and her. They never knew the delights of a daily walk with the Lord—only the stern disciplines. We must all experience the delights of walking in his presence daily; then the disciplines actually become delights.

THE TRUTH BEHIND THE GOLDEN RULE

Do you remember the Golden Rule? "In everything, do to others what you would have them do to you" (Mt 7:12). The Golden Rule says, "Decide what you want others to do to you, then first do that to them." It does not say, "Do unto others *so that* they will do unto you." Nor does it say, "Do unto others *as they do* unto you."

The message is clear: our conduct to others is what we want others' conduct to be toward us. The Golden Rule is most golden in our own homes with our own families.

In summary, here are three simple guidelines for Christian parents in helping children become what you want them to be (and what you think God wants them to be):

1. As early as possible in your child's life, decide what you want your child to become, not vocationally but personally, and commit these goals into writing.

2. Make these your own personal goals so that your child will see you live them out each day as a role model.

3. Develop conversations in the context of the delights of daily living, focusing on these goals. Each day learn to talk about these things rather than trivia only. Of course you will also talk about trivia, for life is filled with trivia, often necessary trivia. But as you live out the goals for your children, and see them lived out in your children's lives, you *will* want to talk about them.

TWO

Antidote to Panicky Parenting

Roger Thompson

Where have all the children gone? I don't mean the battery-driven ones who spend their days and nights propped up before the TVs and computer terminals, or the thirty-five-year-old minds in children's bodies, who operate a microwave oven and have their own door key before they're six. Or the ones who log ten thousand jet miles a year visiting two sets of parents. I'm talking about the children who used to enjoy a couple of years of doing nothing but discovering things around them: exploring their curiosity, easing into a family, and being loved. It had a name; we called it "childhood." . . .

Where have all the children gone? They've passed childhood and proceeded directly to adulthood. Realistically, that's where all the action is today, anyway. Young children, more than any single group, have had to bear the brunt of the changes of our society, our mobility, our redefined family structure, our changing technology, and new attitudes toward everything, including them. Children no longer are a dominant force, an excuse, a reason, a goal, a status, or a commitment; they are just there.

—Erma Bombeck, humor columnist

9

N OT ALL OF ERMA BOMBECK'S points are humorous. In this excerpt, she's put her finger on an issue of tragic proportions in our society. Perhaps the problem she points out has crept into our churches and even our homes. This isn't a problem just for unconcerned parents; it's also a problem for people who care about children, who buy books about *Keeping Your Kids Christian*.

CHILDHOOD LOST

I believe, and many others will stand with me, that children in our society learn too much too soon. They watch the same programs as adults do. They see the same discussions on TV about sex and violence, and on the news about AIDS and homosexuality. They hear the platforms of the candidates, and they worry about our world. They learn adult secrets at a very early age. Rare is the pre-teen who evidences what I believe to be the basic gift of childhood, and that is innocence and carefree play. Very rare.

Neil Postman in his book *The Disappearance of Childhood* said,

> One doesn't have to go to exotic sources or evidence. If you look at the tastes and clothing, language, sexuality, and criminal activity of our children, you find them becoming more and more indistinguishable from adults. Childhood as a specific category of people is moving toward extinction.

For instance, children's sports have been professionalized. Witness the Pop Warner National Academic Football Championships played in Alexander City, Alabama, known as "The Kids' Super Bowl." Now these games mimic their adult counterparts: complete with people like Edie Adams singing the national anthem, and with promotional gimicks like astronaut appearances or stunt flyers doing pregame acrobatics.

An article recently published in *The Oregonian* revealed that Max Factor, Revlon, Clairol, L'Oreal, and Vidal Sassoon are creating make-up and beauty care products for younger and younger buyers. They say that the target age to enter the market is now nine years of age. One of the spokesmen says, "By the time they are twelve years old, these girls will be among the highest users of fragrance." There's fierce competition to look right—even among preteens.

Now let me hasten to add, I'm not against hairspray or football. Those are symptoms, symptoms of a much deeper danger for our children. That danger is that we are imposing adulthood on children in this society before they are spiritually, emotionally, and physically able to handle it.

THE SOURCE OF THE PROBLEM

The problem is not with children; it's with parents. When children are used as status symbols, when children are seen as partners, when children are decision-makers in the home over major policy issues, or when children become thera- pists to an upset parent, something is drastically wrong for the child and for the parent. Often we are driven by an obsessive need to see our children excel, take responsibility for themselves, make the right choices, and take on the burden of being "little adults."

You know, the message of the Bible really is not very complex and it applies perfectly to this kind of parenting problem. The message of the Bible is this: God is God, and I am not. It's simple, but even I have trouble remembering it. I'm just a parent, I'm not expected to be God.

Psalm 127 states: "Unless the Lord builds the house, its builders labor in vain. Unless the Lord watches over the city, the watchmen stand guard in vain. In vain you rise early and stay up late, toiling for food to eat—for he grants sleep to those he loves.''

The psalmist is clearly showing in these two verses that *he* understands that God is God and he is not. Not in the task of building a home or a church, not in the task of doing anything earthly, and especially not in building the lives of people we love, are we expected to be God. But the symptom that I often see among parents is panic. And so today we have a new kind of syndrome in our country: it's the overconcerned hyperparent, the panic-stricken parent who feels *some golden opportunity will be missed at age six, and my kid will be a failure the rest of his or her life.* We are being overwhelmed with, consumed with, the responsibility of parenting. We're deathly afraid that we'll end up with some dumb, unathletic, frumpy eighteen-year-old on our hands. But let's face it: How many of you did not bloom until you were thirty? There's a lot of time to grow up.

Now I'm not saying that we live in a perpetual state of panic. I am saying, don't we all have a twinge when some child prodigy the age of our children has mastered the harpsichord, or when some boy your son's age is now the newest frozen yogurt tycoon on Wall Street? Aren't we all driven by a fear of missed opportunities? "Hey, my kid is ten, and he's not been in a Little League World Series, and he hasn't been on a nationally syndicated game show, and he hasn't even been to Space Camp, for goodness' sake.''

Scripture puts a different condition on parenting in Psalm 127. Who is the builder? Is it TV? Is it Madison Avenue? The question is, "Is the Lord building your house, your family?'' If not, the Scripture says three times in the first two verses, "it's in vain, in vain, in vain.'' We can't work hard enough to make it succeed. We can't guard it with enough vigilance. We'll never even sleep soundly unless we accept this condition and let God be the builder of our children.

We're not designed for nor will we ever attain perfect parenthood. The psalmist is reminding us of something so simple: turning the responsibility back over to God. Instead of being panic-stricken, let's let God have his way in our families.

A CONSEQUENCE: BURNOUT

One author has written a book called *Parent Burnout.* What causes it? Seeking perfection is one cause, responsibility without control is another. When a person holds himself responsible for something beyond his control, the probability is certain that he'll experience stress. If a child does something wrong, this kind of parent we're talking about has a tendency to say, "What did *I* do wrong?" That's a good question, but it's *a* good question, not the *only* question that needs to be asked.

Do you hear the peaceful soothing of Psalm 127: "Unless the Lord builds the house"? God is God, and you and I are not. We have a big responsibility, and we need to handle it well, but there's a difference between being responsible for everything that child does and being responsible to our Master who is the Father himself.

Antidotes. Let me give you three antidotes to this panicky parenting.

1. Pray. Just place yourself before God, and realize first who he is. Then recognize this: if my children are going to serve the Lord, if they're going to grow to be what I want them to be and what God wants them to be, they need something more than what I am. Next, pray for your children. By the age of two, there are so many kinds of influence on them: television, school, and friends. Pray for the effect of these influences on the child's heart.

2. Read and listen. Good tapes are available on parenting. Or perhaps you could listen to family-oriented radio programs like Dr. James Dobson's "Focus on the Family." Good information can help us avoid the tendency to parent by trends and not by truth. We can be helped to recognize the difference between facts and myths. For instance, there's absolutely no evidence that if your child reads by the age of three he or she will be a genius in senior high. We can learn to do more than just ask, "What are my neighbors doing? What does the school want me to do?"

3. *Let your kids be kids.* Play is the language of the child. It gives the child a sense of adequacy, of control over his or her world. Play is the work of a child, and children should be allowed to play (I'm not talking about your 16-year-old; I'm talking about pre-teens).

Let your kids be kids. Let them do some disorganized things, and don't force them always to be in organized classes and leagues.

WHO OWNS OUR KIDS

Appreciate the gift of your children.

Sons are a heritage from the Lord, children a reward from him. Like arrows in the hands of a warrior are sons born in one's youth. Blessed is the man whose quiver is full of them. They will not be put to shame when they contend with their enemies in the gate. Ps 127:3-5

The second symptom of panicky parenting I see is in contrast to this awe and appreciation of God's gift of children. What I see in parents today is possession and good old-fashioned selfishness. As a parent I am also subject to it. It's very easy for me to possess my children and forget they're a gift from God. The fact is, they're not mine, but only on loan to me for a period. One day the Master is going to stand me before him and ask, "Roger, what did you do with the inheritance I gave you—your children Jill and Shelley?" And the Master is going to hold Joanne and me accountable for what we have done. He will do the same with you.

The basic issue of parenting is not to forget who owns the kids. The Psalm says they're a heritage—not something owed to us but something given freely by the Master, out of the magnanimity of his heart. It says that children are given as a reward, not because we've earned it, but just because God wanted to give us a present. Those of you who have wrestled deeply with the agony of childlessness know, perhaps better than the rest of us, how precious is the gift of a child.

WHAT PARENTING IS DESIGNED TO DO

David Elkind says, "If it is to be done well, child-rearing requires, more than most activities of life, a decentering from one's own needs and perspectives." As parents, we are not given children so that *our* needs will be met. We are given children because God has blessed us, and now through us our children's needs are to be met. Not the needs that the children say they have, but the needs God says they have.

Children are not given for us to achieve status or vicarious success. They are given to us so that we can value them for who they are and, present them back to God as his stewards. Again quoting Elkind, "When young people assume that parents are concerned only with how well they do rather than who they are, the need to achieve becomes addictive. When children feel that achievement is for the parents, not for self, they either eventually give up or go into achievement overload, and we produce little Type-A performers."

Children don't need to find their worth in performance. Take this comment by a little girl—her name's Martha Taft.

She says, "My name is Martha Bowers Taft. My great-grandfather was president of the United States. My grandfather was a United States senator, my daddy is ambassador to Ireland, and I am a Brownie."

So what is parenting designed to do? Psalm 127 tells us that children are "like arrows in the hand of a warrior." What does that metaphor suggest? An arrow, unlike a sword, can go where the warrior cannot. Children are described as offensive weapons that the parent ought to mobilize to go fight battles that are still far off. The implication is that God knows how to deploy them best, and he is the one who has equipped them with their capabilities.

Parents, we are to straighten the arrows through discipline. We are to sharpen the arrows through instruction. And we are to aim the children by talking about faith and vision with them. "Son, have you ever thought that God could use that skill you're developing in the fifth grade for his cause around the world?" "Sweetheart, have you ever thought that that talent you have for the flute could be used for the Master someday?" "Have you thought, kids, that the kinds of skills you've gained from having a lemonade stand could help you be honorable people in business someday?" Parents are to talk about the future for the Master's use.

But then an arrow has to be let go. That's what parenting is all about. I want to tell you I'm more attached to my kids now than I was when they were a month old. And I'll be more attached to them when they're 16 than I am when they're 8, because I delight in my children, and I want to hang on to my kids. But parenting has as its ultimate goal letting them go. Children are arrows, not swords.

I think about the family into which I married. The Joneses had six children, and those six children were released to marry six Christian spouses. And out of that are eleven or so grandchildren. So out of two faithful people who were willing to release, there's now potential for almost twenty-four people serving Jesus Christ.

Psalm 127 verse 5 says, "Blessed is the man whose quiver is full of them. They will not be put to shame when they contend with *their* enemies in the gate." The word is *their:* not mine, not yours, but our children's enemies. How do I equip a child to meet his or her enemy down the road? I have to say, "Child, I have you for this time, and my task is to take your hand and slip it out of mine and put it into the hand of God. I'm here to train you to look upward for your strength. I'm here to help you see that God is God and you are not." The battles that I face today will not be the battles my daughters will have to fight later. I'm to equip my children, under God's hand, as a steward, to meet demands that I have never perceived.

Children are to be let go, and they are to be equipped. The Bible calls it "leaving and cleaving." The Psalm makes it very clear: we can't hold them. They're not here to fight our battles, but to fight new battles that the Master will deploy them to fight—in their world, without me, without you.

What are your children learning? I can't be the Holy Spirit for you. I can't tell you what to take and what to leave, what to start up and what to let go. But God will show you. Let the Lord build your house, and allow God to come and meet with you as a parent so that his purposes are met in your home.

THREE

How Responsible Are Parents for a Child's Behavior?

James C. Dobson

"WHAT KIND OF PARENTS ARE YOU not to have any more control over your son?" Perhaps the exact words differed, but the message came through loud and clear as they sat in front of the pastor, the minister of education, and the board members of the Christian school to request that their son not be expelled with only six weeks of school left.

"We've been Christians for seven years, and we've done everything possible to help this child, from prayer, to moving this past year, to putting him in a Christian school, to weekly family counseling sessions," the mother wrote to me. "We are failures at parenting. Please help. We are desperate!"

If we talked to the minister of education, we might hear a different story about these parents and their rebellious son. Perhaps they did cause his defiant behavior, but I doubt it. Their four other children were doing fine. No, I think they were victims of the cruel notion that parents are responsible for everything their child becomes.

THE MYTH OF DETERMINISM

Contemporary parents have been taught that children are born neutral and good. If the children go wrong, it is because someone wreaks havoc upon them. All behavior is *caused,* say the experts. The child chooses nothing. He merely responds to his experiences.

This theory is called "determinism," and if it is valid, then the responsibility for every lie, every school failure, every act of defiance eventually circles around to his family.

I remember boarding a plane a few years ago for a trip from Los Angeles to Toronto. A mother sat down two seats from me and placed her three-year-old son between us. *Oh boy!* I thought. *I get to spend five hours strapped next to this little live wire.*

To my surprise, the toddler sat pleasantly. He sang, played with the ashtray, engaged himself in thought, and slept. His mother acted as though all three-year-olds were able to sit for half a day with nothing interesting to do.

A few months later on another flight, I was seated across from a well-dressed woman and her very ambitious two-year-old girl. In a few minutes, the flight attendant came by and urged the mother to buckle the child down. The two-year-old was kicking, sobbing, screaming, and writhing for freedom! Begging her child to settle down, the mortified mother hung onto her with all her strength. Once we were airborne, she released the little fireball, covered her face with both hands, and wept.

How did the mothers on these two airplanes probably feel about themselves and their very different toddlers? I would guess the woman with the passive little boy was significantly overconfident; she couldn't understand why others find child-rearing so difficult. The mother of the second toddler was almost certainly experiencing a great crisis of confidence; she wondered how she had managed to make such a mess of parenting in two short years.

At least part of the problem resided in the child's temperament. But my point here is this: parents today are much too willing to blame themselves for everything their children do. Only in this century have they been so inclined. If a kid went bad one hundred years ago, he was a bad kid. Now it's the fault of his parents.

I know that our society today is peppered with terrible parents who don't care about their kids. Some are addicted to alcohol, gambling, pornography, physically or sexually abusive behavior, or just plain selfishness. I'm not writing to soothe their guilt.

But there are others who care passionately about their sons and daughters, and they do the best they can to raise them properly. Nevertheless, when their kids entangle themselves in sin and heartache, guess who feels responsible for it?

This tendency to assume the responsibility for everything our children do is not only a product of psychological mumbo jumbo (determinism), but also reflects our vulnerabilities as parents. We know we are flawed. We know how often we fail. And all our shortcomings are magnified tenfold when a son or daughter goes bad.

WHAT SCRIPTURE REALLY SAYS

The inclination toward self-condemnation also reflects the way Christians have been taught to believe. Though I am not a theologian, it is apparent to me that a serious misunderstanding of several key passages has occurred. The error has produced false condemnation for circumstances that exceed parental control or influence.

How do you interpret Proverbs 22:6, which says, "Train up a child in the way he should go, and when he is old he will not turn from it?" Does that verse mean that the children of wise and dedicated Christian parents will never be lost?

I wish Solomon's message to us could be interpreted that confidently. The common understanding of the passage is to accept it as a divine guarantee, but it was not expressed in that context.

Psychiatrist John White, writing in his excellent book *Parents in Pain*, has helped me understand that the Proverbs were never intended to be absolute promises from God. Instead, they are *probabilities* of things that are likely to occur. Solomon's purpose in writing the Proverbs was to convey his divinely inspired observations on the way human nature and God's universe work. A given set of circumstances can be expected to produce certain consequences.

Several of these observations, including Proverbs 22:6, have been lifted out of that context and made to stand alone as promises from God. If we insist on that interpretation, then we must explain why so many other Proverbs do not inevitably prove accurate. For example: "Lazy hands make a man poor, but diligent hands bring wealth" (Prv 10:4). Have you ever met a diligent—but poor—Christian? I certainly have.

Obviously, the humanistic concept of determinism has even found its way into the interpretation of Scripture. Those who believe Proverbs 22:6 offers a guarantee of salvation for the next generation have assumed, in essence, that a child can be programmed so thoroughly as to *determine* his course. The assignment for parents is to bring him up "in the way that he should go."

But think about that for a moment. Didn't the great Creator handle Adam and Eve with infinite wisdom and love? He made no mistakes in "fathering" them. They were also harbored in a perfect environment, with none of the pressures we face. They had no in-law problems, no monetary needs, no frustrating employers, no television, no pornography, no alcohol or drugs, no peer pressure, and no sorrow. They had no excuses! Nevertheless, they ignored the explicit warning from God and stumbled into sin.

Ezekiel 18 is helpful to us in assessing blame for the sinful behavior of grown children. God's way of looking at that situation is abundantly clear:

> The word of the Lord came to me: What do you people mean by quoting this proverb about the land of Israel: "The fathers eat sour grapes, and the children's teeth are set on edge"? As surely as I live, declares the Sovereign Lord, you will no longer quote this proverb in Israel. For every living soul belongs to me, the father as well as the son—both alike belong to me. The soul who sins is the one who will die. Ez 18:1-4

Then in verse 20 he concludes: "The son will not share the guilt of the father, nor will the father share the guilt of the son. The righteousness of the righteous man will be credited to him, and the wickedness of the wicked will be charged against him."

These words from the Lord should end the controversy once and for all. Each adult is responsible for his own behavior, and that of no one else.

God did not intend for the total responsibility for sin in the next generation to fall on the backs of vulnerable parents. We find no support in the Bible for that extreme position. Cain's murder of Abel was not blamed on his parents. Joseph was a godly man and his brothers were rascals, yet their parents were not held accountable for the differences between them. The saintly Samuel raised rebellious children, yet he was not charged with their sin.

In the New Testament, the father of the Prodigal Son was never accused of raising his adventuresome son improperly. The boy was apparently old enough to make his own headstrong decision, and his father did not stand in his way. This good man never repented of any wrongdoing—nor did he need to.

It is not my desire to let parents off the hook when they have been slovenly or uncommitted during their child-rearing years. There is at least one biblical example of God's wrath falling on a father who failed to discipline and train his sons. In the First Book of Samuel 2:22-36, Eli, the priest, permitted his two grown boys to desecrate the temple. All three were sentenced to death by the Lord.

Obviously, God takes our parenting tasks seriously and expects us to do likewise. But he does not intend for us to grovel in guilt for circumstances beyond our control.

A RESOURCE FOR IMPERFECT PARENTS

So where does this leave us as Christian parents? Are we without spiritual resources with which to support our sons and daughters? Absolutely not! We are given the powerful weapon of intercessory prayer.

The Scriptures teach that we can pray effectively for one another and that such a petition "availeth much" (Jas 5:16 KJV). God's answer to our requests will not remove the freedom of choice from our children, but he will grant them clarity and understanding in charting their own course. They will be given every opportunity to make the right decisions regarding matters of eternal significance.

I also believe the Lord will place key individuals in the paths of the ones for whom we pray—people of influence who can nudge them in the right direction. Shirley and I prayed this prayer for our son and daughter throughout their developmental years: "Be there, Father, in the moment of decision when two paths present themselves to our children. Especially during that time when they are beyond our direct influence, send others who will help them do what is righteous and just."

The past is the past. You can't undo your mistakes. You could no more be a perfect parent than you could be a perfect human being. Let your guilt do the work God intended, and then file it away forever. Pray for your children in confidence—not in regret. I'll bet Solomon would agree with that advice.

Part 2

Keeping Your Family Christian

FOUR

Creating a Christian Home Life

Gordon MacDonald

E LI WAS A ROTTEN FATHER. The first two shots he took at raising boys were an abysmal failure, and he gave the world two monsters. So God must be a gracious God, because he gave Eli a third chance. When Hannah and Elkanah presented their precious young son for service at the temple, this time Eli performed.

What was Eli's mission in the raising of Samuel? His mission was to raise Samuel to recognize God's voice. When God spoke after years of silence, Samuel knew (with Eli's help) who was calling him and how to respond. There could be no greater mark of success for the man who is privileged to be called father.

Any healthy male past the age of puberty can become a father, but it takes a man who understands *his* mission to succeed at it. The mission of any Christian father is to raise children in such a way that, like Samuel, they may be able to recognize the voice of God and respond appropriately. Although this encounter happened in the tabernacle at Shiloh, God wants to encounter fathers and their children today.

Gail and I and our children, Mark and Kristi, lived for thirteen years on Grant Street in Lexington, Massachusetts. Our house was a small, ranch-style home with six or seven rooms and one bathroom. (We shake our heads when we realize we raised a family with one john.) Before we said our final good-bye and moved from Grant Street, I said to my wife, "Why don't we go back into the house one more time? Let's tour each room and see if we can form one final memory of something that happened so we can carry it with us." And so we went from room to room and decided the most memorable experiences that had happened in the vocation of mothering and fathering during those thirteen years.

THE BREEZEWAY: FAMILY MEANS BUILDING

The first room is the breezeway, sometimes the family room. I remember coming home one day when our children were around the ages of nine and six. As I entered the breezeway, the two of them were standing nose-to-nose, ripping each other apart. I was amazed at the words and the anger. I was grieved, as any father would be watching his children fighting with each other. Putting my hands on their shoulders to separate them, I said, "Listen carefully. This place is called *home*. It is unlike any other place. When you enter into a home, people do things differently. In a home, they build each other. Did you hear that word? They *build* each other. Outside that door, people carve each other up. They compete with each other. And sometimes you have to look over your shoulder to see who may be coming up behind you. You should never have to do that in a home. I anticipate from this moment forward that the content of your conversation will always be in the mode of *building,* because here we are growing human beings to the glory of God."

Our cliche became *build.* It came home to roost one day

when I said an idle word to my wife and one of our children said to me, "Now Dad, was that a building statement? Why don't you say it again to Mom and see if the second time you can do it right?"

I believe one day those men entrusted with wives and children will stand before God, and among the first questions he might ask would be, "Did your child and spouse grow to be all that I designed them to be in the environment you created?" In the breezeway, the great memory was the admonition *to build.*

KITCHEN: LEARNING TO PUT FAMILY FIRST

You go from the breezeway to the kitchen. At one end was a lovely old table we had refinished, and around that table we ate our meals. When it was time to eat, the phone came off the hook because for the hour we were together, the family was the ultimate priority. That did not happen by accident, for as our children began to enter the preteen years, Gail and I discovered that our family schedule was falling into the hands of everybody outside the house. The children were victimized in a positive sense by the wonderful things to do in the school. The church had its own programs. The community had its programs. If we did not have control of our family calendar, before long we would be going in four different directions, having almost no useful time together.

One day my wife made an announcement with my support. She said, "From this day forward, every evening at supper time, we are going to eat together. It is an inviolable part of the daily schedule. I don't care what time we eat, as long as you tell me when you can all be here." My contribution was to suggest that supper time was meant for more than eating, it was meant to be a relational event.

That, I believe, is the second mark of a home, its members learn to talk with each other. No one will learn to talk if the time is not taken and if interruptions are not minimized. As we stood in the kitchen of the empty house, my wife and I began to recall great conversations that happened around that old table. The evenings when one of the children came home defeated in an event at school and needed an opportunity to give vent to feelings and frustrations, or stimulated by interesting questions merged into long conversations about sex, about marriage, or how you hear the voice of God.

If your children are anything like mine, they don't like to talk. "How was your day?" "Good." "Is that all, good?" "Yeah." "But, that's the way it was yesterday, and the day before that." So fathers have to be creative, like, "If you don't tell me what was the most interesting part of your day, it will cost you a quarter." Sometimes it takes a father who admits to his children that he also had struggles that day, or that he has failed. But sooner or later, because the time is taken, families learn to talk.

DECISIONS IN THE LIVING ROOM

When you leave the kitchen, you come to the living room. Our living room had a large plate glass window, and my memory as I entered that room was of our daughter, Kristi, who often sat on the love seat looking out the window. I often saw her there at 5:30 in the morning, when, for an hour with her Bible and journal, she would spend time ordering her world and bringing it into reconciliation with God.

She often did her homework out there. The living room was a lovely place, and Kristi liked it very much. But one Saturday afternoon, Kristi sat in front of that window, and I knew the thoughts this time were difficult thoughts. Gail had put me on to the fact that Kristi was struggling, and maybe it was time for her father to enter the act. This issue was simple. She had to make a big decision as to where she was going to attend high school. One group of friends thought she ought to go to the public school, and the other group thought she ought to go to the Christian school. She knew that to make a decision would hurt one group. Here was a fourteen-year-old child, more girl than woman, wrestling with a massive decision.

As I listened to her talk, I finally heard myself saying, "Kristi, all men and women, be they teenagers or adults, have moments when they are like an oak tree or a tulip. The trick is to know which you are. Oak trees grow and stand tall. They take a long time, but when they get to full growth, no one messes with them. You walk around them, because oak trees stand by themselves, strong and beautiful and tall. And Kristi, I have seen you when you are an oak tree. On the other hand, tulips grow to fullness and beauty also, but even at their greatest height and beauty, they need to be protected. You need to build a fence around a tulip, but you don't have to worry about an oak tree at all. So, it's important for fathers to ask their daughters, 'Are you today an oak tree or a tulip?' because if you are an oak tree, Kris, I'll leave you alone. But if you are a tulip, I'll build a fence around you today."

She pondered the alternatives, and then came the tears and finally the quiet voice, "Daddy, today I'm a tulip." With those code words, a father knows it's time to protect. Thank God, there are moments when fathers have that opportunity to build a fence. And thank God for the moment when he gives us the spirit of discernment to know when our children need the fence because they are tulips and when we need to stand aside because they are becoming oak trees.

A BEDROOM WITH FLEXIBLE STRENGTH

If you walk down the hall, there's a bedroom where our son, Mark, lived. And now a memory quickly came to me. Mark was a sixth grader when the event happened. He had rushed in the door of our home after school and said, "The kids have asked me to go with them to Cape Cod this weekend. There are fourteen of us going, seven boys and seven girls. It's going to be fantastic!" Sixth grade. I took one look at him and with all my good interventive techniques, said, "No way!" Sixth grade is generally the year when boys and girls form peer groups, when popularity becomes an issue, when being in the in-group is the most important thing in the world. To be invited to go to the Cape for a weekend is a special privilege, and to hear from your parents that there's "no way" is devastating.

Mark quickly disappeared, and for a half-hour I didn't hear anything from him. I began to search the house, but I couldn't find him. Then suddenly I realized there was something unusual about the bedroom—the closet door had been shut. So I went back and opened that door. There, back in the corner, was my son, sitting with his knees wrapped up to his chest, quietly weeping. I'd never seen him do that before.

There aren't textbooks that tell a father how to perform in a moment like that, but instinct told me I ought to join him. I found myself closing the closet door behind me and getting down on the floor in that darkened closet. I sat in the darkness for ten minutes and listened to my little boy weep. Finally, when there were no more tears, I began to rethink the decision I had made and whether I had been too arbitrary. "Son," I said, "let's talk. It's obviously very important to you. Tell me about the ground rules. Tell me what's going to happen." And with that, the story came out, the story I had been too gruff to listen to. When he finished, I said, "Bud, I'll back off. You go. But I want you to promise you will watch everything that happens this weekend. Watch the way the adults act and the way they treat their son. Watch the way the young people treat each other. Promise that the minute you get back, the two of us will sit down and have a long talk about everything you saw and how you felt about it."

He said, "Dad, I promise." He went, and (thank God) he had a thoroughly miserable time. "It was crazy, Dad. Those parents didn't care what their kids did. The kids were left on their own, hour after hour. Something wrong could have gone on. You and Mom would have never acted that way. I'm really pleased that you let me experience that, because I saw how different families treat each other." From that weekend, because I made a choice to flex as a father, my son and I had a different relationship, which lasts until this day. He learned and I learned that part of good fathering, in addition to holding principles and convictions, is to learn to negotiate and flex. A father must sometimes allow his son or daughter to take a few chances for the possibility of learning valuable lessons on their own.

THE HEART-TO-HEART BEDROOM

Down the hall is the bedroom where Gail and I lived. When we reached that room, we laughed a bit as we remembered that it was to that room late in the hours of the night that the children often came with all sorts of wonderful and troubling stories.

There was the night at 12:30 when a soft knock came on the door and a rather quiet male voice said, "Dad, can I come in for a moment?" The door opens and our son walks in at the age of seventeen. He's breathing hard. He says, "Dad, I don't know how you are going to take this, but I got a speeding ticket tonight. You warned me, and I've gotten it and I'm very, very sorry." And he sits on the edge of the bed and he talks about how he made the mistake. You say to yourself, "Thank God we have achieved a point where the boy can admit he's wrong." We talk about what we're going to do about it. We give each other an embrace, and he goes to his bed.

Or there was the night when the same kind of knock came on the door, and this time it was a feminine voice: "Daddy? Mom? Can I come in?" And a little girl now turned seventeen sits on the edge of the bed and tells you about a handsome guy she has met, and how he has feelings for her, and she has feelings for him. You look mesmerized as the little girl unfolds the fact that now she has become a woman, her heart has been captured. Just two weeks ago I walked her down the aisle to commit herself to that young man. But there in that bedroom, we heard the story of their budding romance for the first time.

Gail and I look at each other in that empty bedroom and remember moments like that when there was the admission of pain and the first seeds of joy, and we say to ourselves, "Thank God, our children knew this was a room to which they could come no matter what the hour to talk about what was in their hearts."

GARAGE CONTINGENCIES

The garage brought to us the memory of a red pickup truck that for many years was housed in it. When our son turned sixteen, the learner's permit was hardly dry or in his billfold when he came to me and said, "Dad, next Friday I have a date. I'd like to take her in the truck." I said, "Well, Bud, you can't do that. You only have a learner's permit, and you can't go out at night without someone who has a license." "Dad, she has a license." "But the licensee has to be eighteen." "Dad, she's eighteen and a half." "Where is the date?" "Boston." "What time does it start?" "Five-thirty." "Have you ever driven in Boston at 5:30 on Friday afternoon?"

I wanted to say, "No way!" but I had learned my lesson. I

said, "Bud, give me two hours to think about it." I went to call the girl's father: "Don, you know your daughter and my son have a date next Friday, don't you?" He said, "Yes, I do." "How would you feel if you knew that Mark was going to drive on that date with just a learner's permit because your daughter has a driver's license?" He said, "Gordon, I trust Mark's judgment. If you feel he should do that, it's fine with me." The two hours were almost gone, and I told my son, "Mark, my answer is yes under one condition. On the night before your date, you and I will drive the route to the date at the same time of day, and you will permit me to create any kind of circumstance and you will have to react to it." He said, "Sure, Dad."

The next Thursday at 5:30, we started out in rush-hour traffic, bumper to bumper. I suddenly said to him, "Son, I'm sorry, but your right front tire just blew out."

"What do you want me to do?"

"What do you do with tires that have just blown out?"

"You change them."

"Then get over there and change it!" So we pulled over into the breakdown lane with me praying that a cop wouldn't stop. Mark climbed under the pickup truck to get the jack. When he reappeared after ten minutes, he didn't have the jack. Mark found out that afternoon that jacks in most pickup trucks are under the hood.

He also discovered what to do when an alternator burns out. He figured out what to do when an exit ramp from the freeway is blocked because of construction, and you have to take an alternate route. He also learned what happens if the truck completely breaks down late at night and you need to decide whether or not to call the girl's father. When we got home that night, I think Mark knew every contingency about driving a pickup truck to Boston on a Friday afternoon.

I smile about that as I stand in the empty garage in the house on Grant Street. But that's the act of fathering. It's releasing the child to face the possibilities and to grow through experience once you have taught him everything that's possible to give him.

THE NOT-SO-HAPPY BIRTHDAY PARTY

The last room we walked through was the dining room, and the memory I have of the dining room is not as happy as all the others. It came the night of a birthday party for me. Gail had cooked my favorite food and decorated a beautiful cake. The presents were all wrapped. The lights were now low, and the family gathered for the supper. But it was clear from the outset that the children were too caught up in their own thoughts to be in sync with the evening's activities. First they got to complaining about a vegetable they didn't like (which I did), and soon they started bickering with each other. Then they sprang up from the table and announced they were going to watch a favorite television show and they'd appreciate it if we'd wait for them. We waited at the table for thirty minutes, me saddened that the kids didn't think my birthday was important. We were even tempted to ask the question parents ask on occasion, "Where did we go wrong?"

Finally after an hour they came up and one said, "Where's the cake? When are we going to open the presents?"

I said, "I'm sorry, the party has been canceled."

"It can't be canceled. This is your birthday."

I said, "I know it's on the calendar, but a party is a party only when the people determine it's supposed to be a party and act in a party mood. Two of the four of us decided today to party by themselves. So maybe we'll have the party in another few nights. But not tonight. The party's over."

It was not a pleasant scene as our children walked away with tears. Later that night, sitting at the edge of the bed with my son and listening to him apologize to God and to his father because of his selfishness, I realized there are moments in the raising of a family when fathers have to make difficult decisions and say and do painful things. In my journal that night, I wrote these words:

> It would be so easy, God, to make simple decisions dictated by convenience and the desire to be liked. But just as I withdraw the hand that offers pain to my children, you remind me, God, that one never learns and grows and blooms when the climate is easy. Teach me therefore, God, like a father to think with eyes and ears, to brood with a heart just like yours, which sees in the scope of eternity's process what makes people, even my children, become like your Son, Christ. The ecstasy of this one moment when simple decisions might bring temporary tranquility is not to be compared with the maturity of all the tomorrows through which my children must live.

For the final time, we locked the door on the house on Grant Street. It's not quite the same place with the furniture gone and the curtains down and the pictures off the wall and the shouts and the joys and even the tears of the children not there any longer. It's just an empty, four-walled structure that a new family will fill with its artifacts in another day or two. A house is not made of drywall, studding, and plate glass windows. No, a house is a place that becomes a home when there is a decision on the part of a father and a mother to make the people inside it grow. And there comes a day when, having grown, the children leave and become what their choices have allowed them to become. As we drive up Grant Street, leaving behind us the empty house, we are able to pray, thanking God that he gave us a home where children grew.

For some of you, that is a dream yet to happen. For others, it's a dream in progress. For many of you, like me, it is a memory. But thank God for fathers who help children and young people hear the voice of God. It is one of the greatest privileges in the world.

FIVE

Building Family Traditions

Gloria Gaither

TRADITION. The very word conjures up pictures of folk festivals, ceremonial dances, and fiddlers on roofs. I hear bands of bagpipes or tom-toms, banjos, and bass fiddles. I see brides with honeysuckle in their hair, jumping with their bridegrooms over ceremonial broomsticks.

I smell Thanksgiving turkey and boiled cranberries, cedar trees, and pumpkin pies. I see pale, freshly churned butter oozing down over thick slices of homemade bread. I see construction paper and doily valentines, bestowed with small soggy kisses. I hear secrets being whispered in the dark on Christmas Eve.

Tradition gives me a feeling of solidarity and roots, a knowing there are *some* things one can count on. Tradition. Priceless heirloom treasures to be taken out and used with reverence and joy, then carefully wrapped and preserved to be passed along to someone else who's dear and special.

I don't know when the erosion began. I don't know just when it was that the rumor started that the treasure was a fake, that the heirlooms should be rooted out and thrown away. But rooted out they were, as someone shouted "NOW! Now is all that counts! The past we must forget. The future doesn't matter. Now! We'll do whatever feels good NOW."

And so with axes, the vandals chopped away the Family Trees and sold the priceless forest of our culture by the cord for firewood. It was not until the inevitable erosion had eaten deep into the ground of our own being that we came to recognize our barren wasteland and long once more for shade and breeze and seedlings nourished by the fallen foliage of the past. Now, almost too late, we have come to recognize the principle of deferred gratification and the need for conservation of the precious resources that nurture and sustain the spirit of mankind.

And that is what we need—nourishment for the spirit, not to be confused with silly sentimentality. Perhaps it was just such confusion that precipitated the present generation's scorn of so-called "tradition." Perhaps some mistook a set of empty and meaningless sentimentalities for truth handed to the young by the wise.

Nevertheless, this generation finds itself sorely in need of meaningful moments that will strengthen relationships and build up moral muscle in our society. We need healthy memories of the past for a clear sight toward the future.

There are too many aimless youngsters who know neither where they've come from nor where they are going. There are too many babies that have been thrown out with the bathwater, while their parents tried in vain to fill their own empty days with immediate thrills to quiet the inner longing for permanence and meaning.

We reap just now the emotional and psychological harvest of a free-love philosophy that has turned out to be neither free nor love. We have found out the hard way that love isn't something one "falls into," but something one *commits* to. We have on our hands a broken culture that has been tricked by the fickle promise of relationships without commitment, of affairs without involvement, and of love without genuine giving of time, energy, and caring.

Where do we as Christian families begin to make a positive difference in our throw-away society? How do we take seriously the command of love without angles, to give of ourselves when there is no promise of material, emotional, or social return? Where do we begin to live out our claim to put value on things that are eternal?

One place we can begin is to put value on time spent together doing things that are meant only for the purpose of celebrating our gratitude for the gift of what God has done in our lives. Praying together spontaneously—giving thanks for a sunset, asking God's help on a math test, praising God for the baby's first step—cultivates an atmosphere of Godness in our homes. There is nothing quite like a spirit of total gratitude to change our view of things and motivate us to see and reach beyond ourselves.

Some neighbors of ours sent the youngest of their three children to vacation Bible School for the first time. One of the crafts he was asked to make there required that he list the number of people in his family. "There are six," he told his teacher. The teacher knew his family of five, and, thinking the little boy was confused about his numbers, suggested that he count again. "No, there are six!" he insisted, and began counting on his fingers. "There's Mommy—Deanie Carroll, and Daddy—Johnny Carroll, Penny Carroll, Marty Carroll, me—Eddie Carroll, and Jesus Carroll!" Being aware that Jesus is a part of the family is a good way to realign priorities.

This awareness of Jesus' presence helps us to say with our time and energy what we say with our mouths. It helps us to value each other in our action. We no longer see time that is not producing income as wasted. We see moments spent listening, talking, playing, and sharing together as the most important time of all. We show our children how much we value such time by passing on to them ideas, celebrations, activities, food, crafts, and literature (books, poems, stories) that were meaningful in shaping our Christian and family values. If we happen not to have had such a heritage, we must create one that our children can remember so as not to leave them impoverished in this important way.

There is no better time than the holidays ("holy" days) to begin to feed the vital root system of our family's growth. Making gifts while talking together about the delight we find in making others happy is an excellent opportunity for building relationships with our own children while instilling values. We can speak often of God's ultimate gift of his Son. We can let our children know, as we remind ourselves, that the joy we have as a family is a direct result of having accepted his gift.

Include the children in doing things for and with older people, shut-ins, neighbors, and persons who serve in the community (postman, pastor, teachers, police, firemen, etc.). Make these activities into traditions with meaning that the whole family can look forward to each year. Let gratitude for what God has done be the center of everything.

While holidays are a good time for building relationships, they are certainly not the only time. There is something in every season, in every day, to celebrate with thanksgiving. Celebrate the creatures God has made, with birdfeeders, berried plants, and protection. Let these be gifts we give in return for nature's gifts to us. Press leaves, save wild flowers, spraypaint weeds, and take time to notice. Together. Make a tradition of walking to church on nice days, or of having Saturday breakfast at McDonald's or of making the first trip of the summer to the Dairy Queen.

Learn to play together with uninhibited delight in each other's presence, freed by the joy of knowing that God is "in the family" loving us, forgiving us, and expecting a new set of values from us.

Today we can do something special with our child that will be a lasting childhood experience on which he or she may build forever.

SIX

Family Devotions They'll Desire—Not Dread!

Craig and Carolyn Williford

"JEREMY AND CHRISTOPHER, let go of the dog's tail and come to the table. No, you *cannot* put his tail in his water bowl. Come on, honey! We're ready to start our family devotions! Christopher! Grab Becky before she drinks out of the dog's—Ugh. Just put her in her highchair, okay, Chris? Now, let's all settle down and . . ."

"Dad, are we gonna hafta listen to 'Daily Dread' again?"

"That's 'Daily *Bread*,' Jeremy. And you should be excited to learn about God! Quit pinching Jeremy, Chris."

"But his feet are under my side of the table!"

"We don't own parts of the table, Chris. Becky, sweetie, don't eat that yucky old cookie from the hinges of your highchair. Jan, don't you ever wash this thing?"

"Of course not; I'm too busy eating bon-bons and . . . Jeremy! Will you just stop that kicking!"

"*Enough already!*" (through gritted teeth) "Now everyone *sit still* and *be quiet* as we enjoy worshiping God as one *happy* family! *Do you hear me*?!"

Silence.

"Dad, are we enjoying this yet?"

43

Do you identify with this scene where noble intentions never seem to meet actual practice? Or has your family been more successful than ours at traditional family devotion? Do you feel—as we did—tremendous pressure and guilt to do family worship and then feel frustration and more guilt when it bombs?

Continually trying to force this routine pattern of devotions was so negative that it was damaging our sons' concepts of worshiping together as a family. When we came to this startling realization, we knew a creative change was a necessity. Therefore, we began a totally new approach to our family worship times: combining traditions, celebrations, worship, creative learning activities, and just plain fun into one unit. The result was integrated, active devotions for our "family that couldn't sit still."

We based our ideas on integration. Since we're both educators and have a strong desire to minister, we have long attempted to integrate our faith into every aspect of our teaching and lives. Yet, our devotional pattern seemed to say, "Sit and listen to this. Now, go out and live in the world." We weren't really picturing the *connection* between the hearing and the doing—*daily* doing. Now, our family devotions and traditions are an active "living picture" of the integration of our faith into the halls at school, the basketball court, and especially at home—where our real Christian character comes out!

For example, we could have given endless eloquent speeches, read numerous Scripture passages on love and moralized from now until our kids' ears dropped off, and they would *still* argue and pester each other unmercifully—something we as parents never do, right? But when we draw names for Secret Pals and they willingly send each other notes of encouragement and candy surprises, we begin to see some hope!

Another time we played the "Gimme Game." Handing out two wrapped presents to each member of the family, we rolled a pair of dice to see what each must do with his or her presents. A number of 5 or 7 meant one must trade with someone else, and the numbers 9, 10 or 11 allowed that person to open one present. Afterwards, there was no need for us to give hypothetical examples of greed, love, giving, grabbing, snatching . . . Anyway, point made!

After a period of time, we noticed that our devotions seemed to fall into one of three categories: worship and traditions; teaching and application of biblical principles and stories; and lastly, just plain fun. Sometimes these do overlap, however. When we celebrated one year in our home, we had a special time of worship for God's providing; we also recalled our favorite humorous moments from the past year.

WORSHIP AND TRADITIONS

Our worship times have become such a regular and special part of the pattern of our lives that they have developed into traditions. (And ones that our kids demand should we temporarily forget any!) Ever since an especially meaningful devotion many years ago, we have made our wedding candle the focal point at nearly all of these occasions. Often we add a smaller candle for each person— turning the lights out—since candles seem to help set a worshipful atmosphere.

On New Year's Eve, Craig read the special "blessings" which he had written for each of our sons. Each year on Resurrection Day we open new "thank-you's" for Jesus; we now have a stack collected over four years which we read each year. We usually have a special dedication for the boys when they begin a new school year and we also like to dedicate each major purchase—a new car, home, dining room table—reminding ourselves that this belongs to God and is to be used to serve him. At Thanksgiving we've had sharing questions. (What are the attitudes and feelings beneath my thankfulness this year?") and also collected representations in a paper sack (my wedding ring represents my thankfulness for our marriage). Christmas, spiritual birthdays, and our anniversary are other meaningful worship times. And we keep looking for "excuses" for more traditions.

TEACHING AND SCRIPTURE APPLICATION

Our second type of devotion teaches a biblical principle or story in an active, creative way. We've learned Scripture while hiking through the woods, enjoying God's creation along the way, and collecting representations of ". . . whatever is true, whatever is noble," (Phil 4:8), etc. Using music in a variety of ways, we've created our own unique instruments (ever heard of a Williford's Woozleum? No? You're missing out!), learned to evaluate music and praised God by singing and playing instruments countless times. Want to teach your kids what the temple was like? Build one with whatever building blocks they enjoy.

Sometimes we've acted out the meanings of words or scriptural principles, like the beautiful meaning of the word *revealed* from 1 Peter 4 (a magic show proved that what appeared to be hidden was there all the time). Our "servant jar" prompts us to serve one another. On World Relief Night once we ate only a meal of rice, complete with chopsticks to add a bit of fun, and gave the money we saved to a hunger agency.

This type of devotion has either developed from our personal devotions or come about from an area of need that we have recognized in our sons' lives. When basketball league presented all types of problems—from getting along with opponents to being a team player rather than the "ball hog," we had Good Sports Night and role-played good and bad examples on the court.

A drama on television prompted a graphic picture of prejudice: we all helped to make a type of cookies that looked just awful. In actuality they tasted quite good, but the point was clearly made that you should not make a decision before the facts are known!

Lately we reviewed the tribes of Israel—who they were, how they traveled, what the Levites did, etc. Did you know that each tribe had its own banner? (Tradition says that the tribe of Judah had a lion on its banner.) Now we Willifords have a banner, too: a white felt flag with an eagle on two circles of red and blue!

Before we leave on family vacations we always feel the need to somehow ensure a reasonable family harmony (is this an oxymoron?). Therefore, we have a tradition entitled "Burying the Grouch," which means that we have a service to bury the most horrible smelling old sock of Dad's—which we name Oscar. The grumpiest person during our trip is presented with that wonderful sock when we return. Needless to say, we're all generally quite motivated to be congenial. After our last trip, we all agreed to give our dog the sock.

JUST FOR FUN

The last type of family activity we enjoy is just plain fun, and our only true purpose is to enjoy each other. We've had scavenger hunts (which included finding a dead bug and yelling, "This family is crazy!"—outside, of course), clue quests (verses from the Bible contain a clue of where to search for the next clue), shoe games (scattering several pairs of shoes in a pile and looking for your own—in the dark), and croquet (indoors during the doldrums of winter with wire wickets, balloons, a soup ladle, meat tenderizer, spatula, and wooden spoon).

To say that these times have only been for fun is really a misnomer, however. There have been countless opportunities for us as parents to demonstrate good sportsmanship when losing or winning a competitive game; to exhibit creativity as we seek new ways to find enjoyment after a long, boring week; and to share just the pure pleasure that comes from the toes (and goes straight to one's heart) of good tummy-hurting, tears-producing laughter. The special bonding that results from these times cannot be manufactured, mass-produced, or "made in an instant." We truly invest in fun times for the richness of the results: an enjoyment of each other that's deep and warm.

STARTING YOUR OWN FAMILY NIGHT

Some of you may be asking, how does my family begin this new format of family worship? First of all, you will need to commit to the concept—and this will take time, effort, and perseverance through the good times and bad. Our commitment needs to be practical concerning how often we can have family devotions. Our schedule allows one night per week, and we feel comfortable with this. Parents with younger children and a less hectic schedule may be able to do more.

Committing also means a night scheduled just like an appointment on the calendar. When we first began full-time ministry in a church, Craig would leave his family night at home blank on his weekly planning calendar. If someone called with a last-minute need, he would quickly scan the days of the week, notice the empty slot, and proceed to fill it in. You guessed it: another family night bites the dust! Now he writes in "family night"—in ink!—because this appointment is too important to miss.

Before beginning, you also need to evaluate your expectations and goals. Are they realistic? Beware of attempting to take on more than you are able to handle; the result is often guilt and a feeling of hopelessness followed by no devotions at all. Your motivation should not be guilt, but instead a true commitment hopefully prompted by the Holy Spirit to attempt to worship God as a family. *This* commitment has the potential to last. Also, be prepared for those devotions that just don't go well, for this *will* happen. Just like anything else worthwhile in life, the greatest efforts do not always guarantee the best results. But even through the failures, our commitment keeps calling us to consider, "Now, what are we going to do next week?"

We've also learned that effective family time does not just happen; we must plan for a quality experience. And this is where the time and effort of the commitment come in, for we often need a good amount of both to prepare for the evening's activities. If we feel ourselves being pulled toward other projects (and it can be anything—from working on the house to reading the newest book), we mentally picture the two most precious gifts which God has entrusted to our care: Robb and Jay. How can we not put genuine effort into these investments?

SEEING THE RESULTS OF FAMILY TRADITIONS

What do we hope to give our children from these traditions and devotions? First, we desire a family that *wants* to be together. The resulting bonding, unity, and "family identity" all combine to give our family a uniqueness that says, "We belong to one another." What a wonderful way to boost a child's self-image—by reminding the child that he or she is special and uniquely needed within the family unit. Also, we want our sons to know that happiness is a decision no matter what the circumstances are around us. Therefore, we add reasons to inject a bit of humor into the day—even to celebrating our dog's birthday—with cupcakes, ice cream, and presents, too! But most of all, our prayer is that our sons will thirst after God. We desire that they know beyond a doubt that seeking to know our Lord is *not* a boring and dull process, but one that affects every area of our lives (and thus is alive and real) and full of the joy that only he can give (whether our experiences bring happiness or pain).

When studying the Israelites, I have often envied the richness of their traditions and feasts. Joshua 4:1-9 seems especially poignant, as they cross the Jordan River to enter the Promised Land. God instructs them to build an altar of twelve stones commemorating this awe-inspiring occasion. And then he says, "In the future, when your children ask you, 'What do these stones mean?' Tell them ... these stones are to be a memorial to the people of Israel forever."

Can't you just picture a family, many years later, passing by the now old altar? The children, curiously attracted to the pile of rocks, point to the altar and inquire, "Father, why are these stones here?" As the father retells the glorious story, the children's senses must have been alive and eager to take in the impressive sight of the awesome stones, the feel of the water at their feet, and most of all, the stirring words of the true story their father recounts. This is a picture of family worship and tradition!

Our dusty wedding candle, with several very average-looking rocks around it, sits on a shelf in our living room. This symbol—a memorial for our family—is a constant reminder to us of God's faithfulness. It forms the core of our call to worship him together. Have you built the "altar" that prompts your children to ask the question, "What does living a Christian life *mean*, Mom and Dad?" Tell them. Show them.

SEVEN

Capturing Those Teachable Moments

Gloria Gaither

CHILDREN ARE LEARNERS. They learn everywhere. They learn sitting down and standing up. They learn wide awake and half-asleep. They take in knowledge through their eyes, ears, noses, taste buds, fingers, feet, and skin.

They learn while parents are teaching, and they learn when parents hope they're not teaching. Children learn from joy; they learn from pain. They learn from hot, cold, work, play, comfort, and discomfort.

Sometimes we adults associate learning with books and Bibles and structured devotionals. But when the books are closed and the lessons are over, children go on learning. No knobs turn off their little minds.

When I am less than the efficient, organized, calm, creative, well-groomed mother I want to be, I wish there *were* switches on our children's minds. But the children go on watching me, seeing how I handle problems, sensing my unguarded reactions, picking up the "vibes" of our home.

I become painfully aware of my failures when I see some shabby action or attitude mirrored in my child. I, too, am learning. God is teaching me that *all* moments are teachable moments. The place to start buying up those moments is with myself.

I've found it helpful to begin my day sitting alone at the feet of the Master Teacher. There is something special about the dawn when the house is quiet and my mind is fresh. If I can spend the day's first moments alone with God, girding my mind with silence, feasting on the Word, listening; I am more ready to greet the day and my family. God and I have a few moments' head start on them.

The second thing I am learning is that if we are to take advantage of those teachable moments, we have to make sure there *are* moments together. Often our expectations of a "normal homelife" don't match the pace of today's real world.

That doesn't mean we resign ourselves to letting the world squeeze our homelife into its mold. It does mean that if we are going to let Christ remold our homes from within, we are going to have to do it *on purpose.*

Once upon a time, working together, eating together, taking walks, having picnics, fishing, hunting, singing, and playing table games were normal. We parents who grew up in a slower, less urbanized society think these things should happen in our home as a matter of course. When they don't, we are bewildered.

There is nothing wrong with our dreams. The problem is our failure to recognize that with busing, school activities, television, commuting, and career parents, these dreamt-of things are not going to "just happen." But they *must* happen if children are to be nurtured.

The warm circle of the family is still the habitat God intended for the nurture and protection of our young. That habitat must be fiercely protected. The things that prey upon the Christian family today may not "huff and puff and blow our houses in," but they are far more threatening than were the big bad wolves of the prairie. And they can destroy a whole lot more than our houses.

One of the meanest bandits of the modern frontier is unrestricted television. While television has many creative, informative programs, much is degenerate, perverted, bleak, and at best a shameful waste of eternal moments. It may be impressive to march to Washington and picket against objectionable programs, but it's a lot more effective to march across the room and switch off the set.

If enough of us Christian parents would discipline our families' viewing habits, the result will be evident in the quality of time spent together in our homes. We will begin to hear each other and sense what each other are feeling instead of becoming noncommunicative, afraid of silence, and terrified by human contact.

Preserving our spiritual habitat takes ingenuity and commitment to shared values. The whole family will have to learn to say no to the things that would destroy what we value most—time and energy for God and each other.

The third important way to shape our children for life— now and forever—is to give them the base of God's Word. Every set of parents has to work out the plan that suits their family best. But somehow, somewhere there has to be a plan for teaching the stories and words of the Bible.

The challenge is to *create* teachable moments. Relating Scripture to real life is one of the best ways, if we parents know the Word and can draw from its resources. Bedtime discussions about the day, the friends at school, the accomplishments and disappointments can find meaning in one or two well-picked verses. Walks in the woods or on the beach can bring life to verses from the Psalms or Isaiah.

An early-morning fishing outing with a sack breakfast can bring a special significance to the calling of the disciples, the nautical allusions Jesus used, or the feeding of the five thousand.

Working together to plant a garden can help lodge in a child's mind both the fellowship of work and the miracle of the seed. The thrill of seeing tulips bloom or tomatoes ripen can give understanding to the Lord's words about harvesting the kind of seeds we plant.

A colorful chart of the verses a child has learned, followed by a family celebration when the child has accumulated twenty memorized portions, can teach that the Word of God is worth the effort.

When we reward only physical, intellectual, and social accomplishments, we teach children false values. Of course we talk about the rewards that most people might not see—the rewards of becoming God's people as the Word becomes a part of us.

Teach a child special verses that apply to his special times. Take snapshots or let him draw pictures. Then mount and date these in a scrapbook with the Bible verses to reinforce his memory.

Negative experiences are also a part of life, and God's Word must be woven into these times too. It is dangerous to teach children that life should always be pleasant, that God is just a miracle machine or a spiritual rabbit's foot to bring us good luck. The Bible teaches instead that God is working to bring us to spiritual maturity.

How we face negative experiences teaches our children a great deal. The death of someone close, illness, disappointing grades, failure to make the team, being betrayed by a friend, loss of a pet, or an accident can be milestones to spiritual and emotional maturity.

With the Word and values of God woven into the fiber of our days, a fourth way to buy up teachable moments is to *make* some moments special. Crazy impromptu picnics, sledding parties, late summer night drives in the country, spur-of-the-moment bonfires, family basketball, volleyball, tennis, or badminton games, horseback riding or hikes, camp-outs and singing—all say to a family in a hundred ways: "Of all the people in the world, I choose to spend my best moments with you. You're my very best friends."

Family traditions are important. Not just Thanksgiving dinner or Christmas Eve, but other things a family can look forward to: Tommy's birthday, the get-together that always celebrates the first strawberries of the season from Grandpa's garden, the Thursday night popcorn-and-apples-party while watching a favorite family show on TV, or the stopping by the Dairy Delight on the way home from church on Sunday night. Any celebration unique to our family implants a special memory.

Children give us parents an excuse for being ourselves, our excuse to laugh and shout and tumble down the hillside. One of our friends, a brilliant attorney, regrets seeing his children growing up because he'll no longer have an excuse to go sledding down the neighborhood hillside.

"The neighbors will think I'm crazy!"

Perhaps that is one reason he has such special children. They have grown up knowing that of all the world, "Dad always liked us best!"

How do we buy up those teachable moments?

- By realizing that since all moments are teachable, we must *become* what we hope to teach;

- By protecting the habitat of our homes;

- By working the essential Word of God into the everyday nitty-gritty of life;

- By making life a celebration of the Lordship of Christ and the value of one another.

There are no easy how-tos. Each family will have to prayerfully find its own way. When it's all said and done, so many of the choices of life are not between the good and the bad, but between the good and the best. Even good things can rob a family.

A sentence from our Sunday bulletin has been singing its way into my days all week. "Saying 'no' may mean that I've said 'yes' to something higher." I want to say yes... but only to the highest and the best.

EIGHT

Raising Children to Love the Church

Luis Palau

H OW ESSENTIAL IS THE LOCAL CHURCH in developing strong, godly families? One man told me the church definitely takes second place in his list of priorities. "Family has to come first," he said. So, he and his family don't attend church regularly anymore.

Is active church participation optional for today's Christian families? Maybe if you have money, health, and a busy schedule, you don't feel your family needs to fellowship with other Christians.

But when the storms of life hit—and they will—suddenly you'll find nobody's there. If you remain shallow in your relationship to your local church, you will lose out on the support of other Christians when you and your kids need it most.

By neglecting to minister within your local church, you also cause other Christians to lose something. The Lord Jesus himself says in John 15 that he is the Vine, and we are connected to him as branches. As a result, through Jesus, we are connected to each other. We are members of his body, the church.

In 1 Corinthians 12:26 we read, "If one part suffers, every part suffers with it; if one part is honored, every part rejoices with it." How you relate or fail to relate to the body of Christ directly affects other Christians. We need each other!

As Christians, we need to plant our family's roots deep into the local church. But how?

1. Make a commitment to your local church. My wife Pat and I and our sons are active members of Cedar Mill Bible Church in Portland, Oregon. Although we travel throughout the Americas, Europe, Asia, and other parts of the world to proclaim the gospel, we're not excused from taking an active part in our home church and being subject to its elders. We feel it's important to consult with them on major decisions involving our family and sometimes even our entire evangelistic team.

My advice to every Christian is the same: attend church regularly. Follow the prescribed procedures to become a member of your local church. Observe the Lord's supper and follow him in baptism. Inform the church leaders that your desire is to become an active member and submit to their authority.

2. Speak well of your church. Even though it has faults, don't allow yourself to develop a critical spirit (1 Cor 1:10). Your church is your "family" in Christ. Defend it! When others grumble about it, remind them to take the matter to the elders, not to the rest of the body. Let your children hear you talking about "our" pastor, "our" elders, "our" deacons, "our" Sunday School, "our" church retreat. This will help them claim the church as their own as they grow older.

Also, speak well of your church by inviting others to attend with you. A church historian found that the average person in a particular denomination currently invites others to church once every twenty-eight years. Surely we can do better than that!

3. Seek to minister within your local church. Ask what you can contribute to the Body of Christ through involvement in your local church. Remember, "to each one the manifestation of the Spirit is given for the common good" (1 Cor 12:7). It isn't enough to know we have spiritual gifts—we must use them!

Beware of the mindset that looks to see if the church will meet your needs. Since when is the church a country club where you pay your dues until you find something more exciting to do?

Instead, the attitude that should characterize us as Christians is love—a love that gives. The Lord Jesus said, "All men will know that you are disciples if you love one another" (Jn 13:35). When my family is ready to leave for church, we take our expectations about what we want to get and leave them home with our dog. Consequently, everything we do receive is a blessing. We're not there to get, but to give.

4. Give financially to support your local church. Although the New Testament doesn't give a fixed percentage for what we should give, it does emphasize the importance of regular giving. In 2 Corinthians, the apostle Paul explains that we should give proportionately (8:12), abundantly (9:6), purposefully (9:7), and cheerfully (9:7).

Although some may be able to give only ten percent of their income to the Lord, others may give much more, depending on their resources and the needs of the church. But the amount we give doesn't impress the Lord. He looks at our reasons for giving and our sacrifices to give, not the amount. Pat and I taught our four sons to tithe from the time they were young. Their small contributions may not have seemed important at the time, but now giving is a regular, exciting part of their lives.

5. Meet the physical needs of your brothers and sisters in Christ. Whatever we do for the least of God's family, we actually do for him (Mt 25:40). Don't wait until someone asks you to help. Take the initiative to visit the sick and elderly. Take food to those facing financial difficulties.

Several years ago, a friend lost his job. Some months later, we heard that his family's house would be taken away if the payments weren't met. They had already sold their vehicles trying to meet their financial obligations. Pat suggested that we pay one of their house payments. We invited others to help, too. Together, as a body, we can support each other in even the most difficult of times.

6. Show hospitality to your church's missionaries. Have you ever invited missionaries home to join your family for dinner? Try it! Missionaries can be fascinating to chat with around the dinner table. And your children will fall more in love with the Lord because of those special visits.

Today my own sons are more outspoken about their faith than either Pat or I were at their age. In part, I believe this has resulted from their friendships with missionaries.

It hasn't always been easy for my family and me to follow these six principles. Because of many other commitments, we sometimes face tremendous pressures to limit our participation in our local church. But Scripture convinces me that if we keep our commitments to our families *and* our churches, we will be the winners in the long run.

NINE

Helping Siblings Love Each Other

Susan Yates

T HE FRONT DOOR SLAMMED SHUT as my son John raced breathlessly into the house. "Allison," he yelled, as he searched for his sixteen-year-old sister. Finding her in the kitchen, he excitedly exclaimed, "I did it! I got a date for homecoming. Please, please get a date and let's doubledate. We can go to dinner together, and I'll even pay for it all," he begged, hardly stopping to breathe.

"That sounds like fun," responded Allison. "Let's see if Charlie wants to."

With her friend Charlie's consent, Allison and her brother began to make plans. Allison helped choose the flowers for John's date. The boys made arrangements to surprise the girls with dinner at a fancy restaurant. Joyful anticipation filled the house for the next several days as my two teens discussed each detail of the evening together.

Watching this scene, I was amazed. Were these the same two kids who used to throw things at each other, who used to lock one another out of each other's room, who had even been overheard saying, "I hate you"? Marveling at God's grace, I turned away so they wouldn't see the tears in my eyes.

One of the greatest joys parents can experience is watching our children become good friends with each other. When we see a big brother comforting a younger brother who has just been excluded from the neighborhood football game, our emotions are touched. When we overhear two teenage sisters giggling as they study Spanish together, our hearts rejoice. We marvel as we think back to earlier years when we were constantly separating toddlers who were fighting, disciplining big brothers who were picking on younger siblings, and wondering if our children would ever become truly good friends with each other.

Raising children who will love each other will not happen automatically. We need a strategy which will enable us to turn the normal rivalries between siblings into genuine friendships. *Respect, service,* and *appreciation* are three key elements which our children must learn if they are to become good friends with each other.

RESPECT

"You dummy!," "You're stupid," and "Oh, shut up," are exclamations we might hear in a typical home of young children. Rescuing a two-year-old from another toddler who just bit him is likely to be a common occurrence in a household with small children. Hitting, pulling hair, and throwing objects at one another are natural inclinations of young children. While this is an exhausting time for the frustrated mother, it is also a crucial time for teaching the small child to respect his siblings.

We found it helpful to explain to our children that these words were unkind and were not permitted in our home. It was alright to disagree with one another, but it was wrong to be rude or to say unkind things about a person. When these words came out, we washed the offensive mouth out with a little soap. It did not take long to make the point.

Learning to use kind words is a positive means of teaching respect. As children learn to say "please" and "thank you," we should praise them. In turn, we can help them praise one another. Reminding a four-year-old to say, "That's such a good picture" to his two-year-old sister encourages affirmation and builds respect.

Not only will we face the challenge of teaching our children to respect each other's person, we must also begin when they are young to teach them to respect one another's property. Small children will naturally enter the big kids' rooms and wreak havoc and destruction. We must let them know that this is not acceptable.

When our twins were small, I simply had to put hooks out of reach on the doors of the older children's bedrooms. We kept them locked to keep the little ones out. As they got bigger, other discipline measures were used to teach them not to damage other people's things.

Positive training involves helping the children learn to ask if they might borrow their sister's book and teaching them to return it to its proper place. Enlisting a toddler to aid in cleaning an older child's room will instill in him a respect for property.

As we train our children in respect, we will be communicating the subtle message that we value each other's person and each other's things.

SERVICE

Service is a second aspect to training in friendship. Our generation is in danger of losing the concept of service. It must be recaptured in our families. Part of training our children in loving one another involves teaching them how to serve each other.

Jesus himself illustrated the greatest act of service when he laid down his life for us. A parent's role is twofold: to provide opportunities for service and to "clue our children in" to the needs of one another.

Family chores provide a wonderful opportunity for our children to learn to serve each other. When our children are small, teaching them to help pick up toys sets the stage for accepting the responsibility of chores as they mature. "I'm proud of you. You did such a good job putting the toys away," will reinforce a cooperative spirit in our child.

When children have specific chores, they learn to be responsible and they learn to help each other out on occasion. We may need to say, "Sweetie, why don't you make your sister's lunch for her today? She's running late." On another day, the favor might be returned.

Working together on projects also offers an opportunity for the children to learn to serve. Encourage a young child to build a block castle for his toddler brother. Assign two children to plan a surprise dessert together for a family meal. In our large family, we've established a homework-helping order. The oldest helps the next oldest, and so on. This greatly relieves the parents, who can no longer do sixth-grade math, as it teaches the children to serve one another.

Sometimes we may need to "clue our children in" about the needs of another child. Recently, my twelve-year-old son was struggling with a problem. I asked his older brother to talk with him and to pray with him. He did, and both were encouraged. A small child might color a picture and write "I love you" on it, then leave it on the pillow of a discouraged older sister. A parent's role is to creatively think of practical ways to help our children serve each other.

APPRECIATION

Our natural tendency is to take one another for granted. It's helpful to think of teaching children appreciation in two areas: appreciation for who they are and for what they do.

As a small child, I remember my Dad saying to me, "Honey, I'm so proud of you." "Why?," I asked. "Because you're mine," he responded.

We appreciate each other simply because we are family. We have a favorite rendition of spin the bottle. When the spinner lands the bottle, she tells the person to whom it is pointing something that she appreciates about him. Libby once appreciated Allison because she let her sleep with her occasionally and didn't get too mad if she wet the bed. In a brief prayer time it's special to have each person thank God for something about the person sitting on her left.

Last spring, we went to our tenth school music festival. Neither Johnny nor I nor the three big kids wanted to go again. Yet the twins were in it, so we all went, and the boys took their sisters flowers. It was special for the girls to be appreciated by their siblings, and it was good for the older kids to learn that they must appreciate the younger ones.

When we train our children in the principles of respect, service, and appreciation, we will not see instant results. We must remember that we are building for the future. Discouragement is inevitable, but as we persevere, we'll see tiny steps of growth.

In the process we can be encouraged by two things that will happen. As we observe, we will notice a subtle weaning of our children from their dependence upon their parents to dependence on each other. Instead of coming to us, our children will begin to go to one another for advice, counsel, and comfort. Loyalty will grow, and as our children enter adulthood, we will have the assurance that they have built solid friendships with each other, which they will have when they no longer have us.

Secondly, as we train our children in these principles, we will be reminded ourselves to be at work on these qualities in our own lives. We are the role models for our children. They will learn the most by observing how we are practicing service, respect, and appreciation. Often I find that I need to ask: Have I thanked my husband for some simple thing he does which I often take for granted? Is there a child whose bed I could make this once because she's overwhelmed with homework? Is there a child who is sad? Perhaps I could put a love note in her lunch box or leave one on her pillow. None of us will ever perfect these principles, yet a blessing of family is that we are all growing in them together.

The homecoming dance was over, and I could hear Allison and John whispering in the hall as they compared notes about their dates. "Thank you Lord," I prayed. "Thank you for little signs of encouragement. Give me the strength to keep training these precious children, and help me to have patience when I do not see immediate results. Thank you for giving me homecoming to remind me that you are at work."

TEN

Single Parenting Can Be Successful

John Trent

I T WAS TERRIBLY HOT, even for an August day in Phoenix. Still, as she stood in the un-air-conditioned room, a cold chill swept over her. "It can't be," she kept saying to herself as she listened to the harsh voice on the other end of the phone. "No Lord, please . . . Not again. . . ."

Five years earlier, she had moved from Indiana after her first husband had walked in the door and casually announced, "I'm leaving you for another woman. And by the way, I've already filed for divorce . . ."

Coming to Arizona had given her a new start, and after a few years, a new romance. With the war over, surely her marriage to a home-coming hero would signal the beginning of better times.

A short season of blessing did follow their marriage. First a son was born, and then a double blessing when twin boys came along. But with the oldest child barely three, and the twins only a few months old, her phone conversation was like replaying a nightmare.

On the other end of the receiver, her second husband's

voice was repeating words she'd heard from the first. Only this time she was staring at three children as she blinked back the tears and listened to the words. . . .

"I'm leaving you. . . . I don't think I ever loved you. . . . We never should have gotten married. . . . Yes, there's someone else. . . ."

No job. No college degree. No family nearby. And no displaced homemaker or "reentry" support groups at the churches or colleges in the city. After all, this was 1952, and divorce and "single parenting" were far from being socially acceptable.

Truthfully, I don't remember what happened that afternoon. I don't remember the tears falling on me and my twin brother as my mother nestled us into diapers and wrestled with the emotions churning inside her. I never saw my older brother crawl into my mother's lap and cry with her when he found out Daddy wouldn't be coming home anymore. But despite the pain my mother suffered then, and the heartache we all endured later, I know for a fact it was a day that changed my brothers and me . . . for good.

Despite her broken heart, my mother made several important decisions that day that paved the way for me to come to know Christ. She decided then and there that, despite the hardship that would be hers for the next two decades, she was going to do everything she could to help her sons come to know their *Heavenly* Father. All three of us are living testimony that my mother's commitment worked— despite the enormous odds against her.

I've never been a single parent, so I can't speak from that side of the fence. But I can share with you three key principles that my mother discovered and put into practice to help us all make it down the difficult road ahead. Was she perfect at it? No, and you don't have to be either. But was she *consistent*? Yes, and that's the key.

MAKE CONTACT POINTS CARING POINTS

In the midst of that stifling Arizona heat, my Mom made a commitment to use every opportunity to encourage us with her love. It didn't matter where we were, who was around, or how tired she was. The world was going to know that she loved us, and we were going to know it too. How did she convey this kind of love that bonded us to her and attracted us to Christ as we grew older?

As the weeks passed, my mother came to realize that if you're serious about building strong relationships, there are at least four crucial times to take advantage of each day. Namely, the first moment she saw us in the morning, when she dropped us off at school, when she first saw us after coming home from work, and finally, the last words she spoke to us at night.

Her first prayer in the morning and her last at night was that she could turn these crucial *"contact points"* into *"caring points"* for each child. Here are two specific ways she did just that.

She used bright eyes to gladden our hearts. There is a Proverb that reads "Bright eyes gladden the heart . . ." (Prv 15:30). What difference do "bright eyes" make? To her three sons—plenty.

Have you ever attended a party, and suddenly come face-to-face with old friends you haven't seen in years? Instantly their eyes light up, and your spirit involuntarily soars as you can "see in their eyes" how much they value your friendship and have genuinely missed you.

My mother made the decision that whenever she saw us at a key "contact point" during the day, she would always greet us with "bright eyes," like we were long-lost friends. For years, I never quite understood why my spirits always lifted the moment I saw my mother. But today I do. While she didn't base her actions on a scientific study, she certainly could have.

Several years ago at the school where I did my doctoral work, I became aware of a group of researchers who were studying what "attracted" people to others. In their study, they chose six women who were judged by a large panel as being equally attractive. These women were then photographed, and the pictures were shown to a group of college students.

After viewing the pictures, these students were asked their opinion as to which *three* ladies seemed the most attractive and that they would most like to get to know. Unbeknownst to the students, just before the pictures were taken, three of the women were given a solution that made their eyes widely dilate. What happened as these students viewed pictures of these "equally attractive" women? The students overwhelmingly rated the three with "bright eyes" as the most beautiful and attractive!

I can't explain exactly what happened inside me as a child when I saw my mother's "bright eyes," but I learned to look forward to them. As we ran to meet her after work, when she dropped us off at school, and especially when she tucked us into bed, we knew we were loved and special—in part because of her bright eyes.

Was she just a "naturally bright-eyed" person? Hardly. I never knew until years later that she would often pull the car over a few blocks from our house after a rough day at work. There at the side of the road, she would bow and ask God to lift the burdens of the day from her long enough for her to make that first meeting with us filled with love and excitement.

In addition, by making sure that the last contact with us at night was made with "bright eyes," that meant that we had to resolve conflicts before we went off to sleep! While I didn't realize it then, my mother was keeping a dangerous emotional killer out of our lives before we went to sleep each night—anger. And in large part, that came because she had made an internal vow that she would have "bright eyes" for us the last thing each night.

There were times when tears filled my mother's eyes. She wasn't afraid to let us see her cry. But consistently at key contact points, her "bright eyes" helped to cement her love in our hearts . . . and open us to the love of our Savior.

She added meaningful touching. In addition to my mother's bright eyes, I also knew that we were in for a big hug at these "contact points" as well. I've got to admit there was a time during our teenage years when we'd bribe her to drop us far enough away from school so our friends wouldn't see her displays of affection. I was on the football and wrestling teams, and I wasn't about to let my teammates see my *Mom* pin a big kiss on me!

Looking back, even when she "made us give her a hug," she was hugging away many hurts. Even in the teenage "macho" stage, she still was wise enough to know that inside our lives were three little boys crying out for love. We weren't always the most receptive sons in the world, but deep down inside we were always thankful. Her willingness to consistently display her affection with *special touch and bright eyes* went a long way in helping us realize there was a God who loved us.

There's a second key ingredient my mother practiced that can help you help your kids find Christ and stay faithful to him.

CREATE A REALISTIC TEAM ENVIRONMENT IN YOUR HOME

Everyone who is a parent knows the feeling. You walk into your four-year-old's bedroom, and it looks like a war zone. Books have been ripped off the shelves and used as frisbees; dolls have been decapitated and left for dead; clothes have been torn out of a neatly made dresser drawer and strewn out like spaghetti. On top of everything, guests are coming in half an hour, and you still have a salad to make and a table to set . . . and now you want to scream!

Sound familiar? One of the common problems many single parents face is feeling overwhelmed with everything that needs to be done. Without the support of a mate, your workload can easily double, and the stress can quadruple. If a single parent adds in a dose of "guilt" over having to make children do "chores," it's a ready-made equation for family friction and frayed relationships.

Early on, my mother realized the value—and necessity—of creating an environment of teamwork in our home. From age three, each of us was given specific responsibilities that we were expected to complete as "family teammates." As we grew older, the responsibilities grew.

Well before our teenage years, my oldest brother did all the yard work, I cooked our meals, and my twin brother did the bookkeeping. Our helping with chores didn't come naturally, and it took time and accountability to build our chores into habits. But she always let us know that as part of the family team, we each had important assignments to complete.

She also knew it was important for us to be a team when it came to family finances. We'd regularly have meetings so she could let us know how we were doing. She'd explain how much she had, and what it needed to be used for.

Money wasn't a plentiful commodity at the Trent household, so at times we did without. That wasn't always easy, but Mom's willingness to be honest with us helped us better understand why there wasn't always enough money for a "designer" label on the clothes, or a spontaneous trip out to dinner. It also allowed us the privilege of praying for something and waiting for God to provide it, instead of being able to instantly run out and purchase it.

Being part of a team did three great things for us:

1. It taught us the value of responsibility. If I didn't cook, we didn't eat; and I would rather have faced a firing squad than two hungry brothers! Each of us learned the value of following through when others were depending on us.

2. It gave us a sense of value and worth. If my older brother did a great job on the lawn one Saturday, Mom was quick to tell him how proud of him she was. That made him feel like he was important, and that without him, we'd lose a valuable, irreplaceable part of our team. Kids need to know they're needed. One of the best ways to communicate that to them is to give them a responsibility that's all theirs.

3. It created a special bond between us. Like many single-parent homes, there were months when there was more month than money. But because we were told repeatedly that we were a family team, we all dug down deeper and pulled together. Even the trying times created a special bond between us.

In each of these experiences, Mom mirrored for us how valuable we are to Christ, the responsibility we have to him to do our part in the Christian life, and the special bond that enduring tough times together creates with him.

FINDING TREASURE IN TRIALS

I'll never forget that day. The piece of paper they handed out in school may have seemed insignificant to everyone else, but to me it represented everything wrong with my world at the time. I remember reading it for the first time, and a stinging pain going right through my heart. The other boys in class were excited and raced home with the news. Not me; the trip home that afternoon was one I dreaded.

My Mom was home early from work that day; she came to the door to greet me. I tried to conceal the hurt, but trying to hide pain from my mother was like trying to hide an elephant in a mailbox. All I could manage to do was hand her the crumpled paper.

I'd been invited to my first "father-son" banquet.

It's moments like these that can punch holes in a single-parent's heart. Particularly when they're working as hard as they can, and trying their best to love their children—and then they get blindsided with something they can't "solve." But instead of letting this "trial" become a pity-party for me or a crushing defeat for her, when the time was right later that night she used it to help me learn an invaluable lesson. Namely, she helped me see that there can be value in looking for good, even in the bad things that happen to us.

The Apostle Paul spoke eloquently to the Romans about that, saying, "And we know that God causes *all things* to work together for good to those who love God, to those who are called according to his purpose" (italics mine) (Rom 8:28). Translated, that means Christians have God's promise that he will take whatever happens to us, no matter how terrible or traumatic, and use it to accomplish good in our lives.

That night, I remember her letting me share my hurts and disappointments. Finally, when I was talked out, she asked me the question, "John, can you think of anything at all that is good about not going to that father-son banquet?" I didn't understand the question. Slowly and patiently, she helped me see what she meant.

On a piece of paper, she had me write down all the negatives involved. "It is humbling not having a father. . . . It isn't fair. . . . Everyone else has a father who is taking them. . . ." And then while it took more work, I was slowly able to list a few positives that were a part of this trial. "God loves me even if I don't get to go to the banquet. . . . Not everyone in the class has a dad who is able—or even willing—to take him. . . . The pain has certainly made me more sensitive to people who are hurting around me. . . ."

I'm not sure where much of the pain went by talking and writing down my feelings, but my mother's lesson on finding value in trials is a necessity in single-parent homes. (By the way, I did get to go to the banquet after all, and I had a great time. A close friend's father called and invited Jeff and me to attend as his "adopted sons" for the night. It was another opportunity to see God's provision even in our problems.)

The book of James tells us that trials are inevitable. It's our attitude toward them that's a choice. My mother never tried to minimize the hurt we felt. But she was wise enough to know that blaming everything on my father who wasn't there would never help . . . but helping us see that God can bring treasure amidst the trials always will.

If there were a "hall of fame" for single parents, I think my mother would be on the cover of the brochure. And in large part, it's because she always labored to make contact points caring points, to create a realistic team environment, and to help us find treasure amid trials.

Single parenting isn't easy; it never will be. The absence of a mate can create tremendous heartache and pressure. *But that doesn't mean single parenting can't be successful.* The fact that I'm writing this article today is living proof a single parent can raise a child to love God and hold on to him—even in the midst of trials.

Part 3

Making the Faith Personal

ELEVEN

How to Lead
a Child to Christ

Luis and Pat Palau

T ODAY MANY PEOPLE BELIEVE that children somehow become
Christians by osmosis. We've met sincere people who
say, "I was born into a Christian family" or, "I've been a
Christian all my life." The unfortunate thing is that they
expect their children's Christian commitment to happen by
itself, and they never talk about the need for accepting Jesus
personally.

Tragically, some people go a step further and resist the
idea of evangelizing children. In our evangelistic crusades in
Europe, we've seen men and women holding back their
own children from going forward to confess the Lord Jesus
as their Savior. We're seeing that trend in America now, too,
as parents don't expose their children to the church because
"they're not old enough."

Other parents don't talk about the issue of salvation with
their children, as if it were just a theological matter for adults
to discuss at church. The message many children are picking
up is: "Wait until you grow up, and then you can make your
decision."

As parents, we need to dispel our children's misconceptions about what it means to be a Christian and demonstrate that we deeply care whether or not they make a genuine commitment to Jesus Christ. We can't *make* that decision for anybody, but as Christian parents we *can* have an active part in leading our sons and daughters to faith in Jesus Christ.

Proverbs 11:30 says, "The fruit of the righteous is a tree of life, and he (or she) who wins souls is wise." It's thrilling to win someone to Jesus Christ. Your wedding day is exciting; your honeymoon is exciting; your first baby is exciting. But the greatest joy you can know is to see your children trust the Lord Jesus as Savior.

The Lord longs to welcome children into his family. "Let the little children come to me," Jesus said, "and do not hinder them, for the kingdom of heaven belongs to such as these" (Mt 19:14). Through our prayers and encouragement, we can have an active part in seeing God work in our children's lives.

BEDSIDE CHATS

We've found that conversations with children about spiritual matters often take place spontaneously . . . especially if you're trying to put them to bed. Maybe they just want to drag out their nighttime routine a little longer, but take advantage of those times when your children want to talk with you.

Our youngest son, Stephen, for instance, wanted to ask a million questions when we'd put him to bed at night. For a while, he was fascinated with heaven: "Where is it?" "Who's there?" "Who'll be waiting?" "If I go first, when will you come?" "If you go first, will you be there when I arrive?" "How are we going to get there?"

Stephen was especially intrigued about how he was going to physically get up to heaven. His brand of childish curiosity forced us to grope for our explanations. "Okay, what's a good illustration of that?" But we've learned that teaching children is a trial-and-error process. If you use an expression that they take in a wrong direction, don't panic. Our mistakes are not going to threaten God's purposes.

ADDRESSING MISCONCEPTIONS

If you say something and later realize your child misunderstood what you meant, don't give up and quit talking with your child about the gospel. Go back and say, "Now remember what we were talking about yesterday?" and readdress the issue in terms they understand. Use illustrations from their lives, from nature, from things they deal with on a daily basis.

Young children are naturally inclined to trust and believe in God. True, they may sometimes absorb wrong concepts about what it means to "ask Jesus into your heart," but there are a hundred other concepts kids also absorb and later say, "Isn't that funny what I thought when I was five?"

There is nothing innately wrong about a child's inadequate concept of God or Christianity. As 1 Corinthians 13:11 says, "When I was a child, I talked like a child, I thought like a child, I reasoned like a child." The Bible doesn't criticize a child's way of thinking. The One who made us knows us. He understands exactly how children think, and doesn't expect us to fully understand the gospel before we commit our lives to Jesus Christ.

COVERING THE BASICS

Our emphasis in explaining the gospel should be that God is our Heavenly Father. That is essential. Instead of initially focusing on sin—"We hurt the Lord when we do wrong things''—we should major on the fact that our Heavenly Father, who is perfect, loves us with an everlasting love.

Yet the issue of sin needs to be addressed. Many have debated about when children develop a sense of guilt and personal responsibility. No one knows, but it can be much earlier than we ever let on. Many young children are sensitive. That sensitivity may be a seed implanted by God in their hearts.

The aim, of course, is to show children that Jesus took our sins on himself. A simple illustration of this is to place an object in your right hand, explaining that that object represents all our sins. When Jesus died on the cross, God took our sins and laid them on his Son. Then place the object in your left hand. Where are those sins now? They're on Jesus, not me. He took them. They were laid on him by God the Father. That illustration can be repeated again and again to get the point across to your child.

TELLING THE GOSPEL STORY

The subject of the cross and crucifixion of Jesus Christ is profoundly moving to children. Don't shy away from it. Of course, our entire life is spent learning intellectually and emotionally what it really means that Jesus took our sins on himself when he hung upon the cross.

We've found that the best approach in teaching about the Lord Jesus is to start at the beginning and proceed chronologically. First, God loves us so much that he entered the human race. He was born to the virgin Mary. Later, as a man, he healed the sick and fed the hungry. Then, he was betrayed, crucified, and buried. Three days later, he rose from the dead and six weeks later went back to heaven. We have seen a stadium full of children sit attentively listening in wonder to that whole story. The most exciting part is when Jesus goes back up to heaven. The angels come down and say that this same Jesus will come back again. There may be fifteen thousand people in the stadium, but that grips you. He's coming back! The graves will be opened, the dead will be raised. We will see him!

Our goal as parents should be to bring up our children in an atmosphere in which trusting Jesus Christ as Savior is natural, and in which they look forward to seeing him.

EXPERIENCES DIFFER

What happens at the point of conversion varies with individuals. But we feel that a person, at some point, should definitely confess the Lord Jesus as Savior. Such an experience is important to help us confirm our commitment to and relationship with the Lord. We need to say the words, inviting Jesus to become *my* Lord. This gives us a sense of security when Satan attacks us with doubts: "How do you know you're a Christian?" Those decision points are especially important for a child to remember.

It's important, though, for a child to remember his or her own experience instead of simply going along with a group or with what parents push. Pat's grandmother brought the gospel into her family and used to tell people that "Patsy prayed to receive Christ when she was three." But that meant nothing to Pat. Now Pat says, "The day I clearly remember trusting Jesus Christ and making sure of my relationship with him took place when I was eight years old." That was *her* experience.

Sometimes we cling to something our child said or did years ago, thinking that proves he or she is a real Christian. But that same child may end up being rebellious and dead to God as a teenager. If we don't see any real movement of God in our daughter's life, we can't afford to cling to the testimony we've been giving for her. She needs to be the one to give it.

As parents, we have to look for signs of spiritual life in our children. Some signs include spontaneously seeing the presence of God in circumstances. Another sign is a concern for others, especially the lost. Also look for continuing, reaffirming decisions as your child grows and matures in Christ and moves into adolescence.

REAFFIRMING DECISIONS

Our two oldest sons, twins Kevin and Keith, made their decisions independently—and regularly! They were praying to receive Jesus as Savior every Sunday. Theologically, we felt uptight about that. But now they each look back and say that they prayed to receive Jesus Christ when they were six years old at Capital City Baptist in Mexico City. They also had confirming decisions in their early teens through the ministry of musician Keith Green.

Children raised in Christian homes often commit their lives to the Lord Jesus several times in different ways as they're growing up. If you ask them when they became a Christian, they'll probably say, "The earliest decision I can remember is . . ." Others, like Billy Graham's wife Ruth, say they can't remember a specific day when they received Christ, but they can't remember a day when they didn't trust him either. We have to recognize that is often the situation of a child growing up in a Christian home. Why should we instill doubt when a child has always loved Jesus and always trusted him?

At one point one of our sons said that he had received the Lord through one of Luis's messages. But several years later, that wasn't the incident that he came back to when giving his testimony. That's why we felt strongly about not giving our sons' testimonies. There may be several parallel decisions in a child's life, all of which are building blocks in his or her Christian experience. What really matters is the decision that stands out in your son or daughter's heart and mind.

Looking back, we both can recall saying to the Lord in our teenage years, "Now Lord, you know that I accepted you years ago ..." but we recommitted our lives to him anyway. As Psalm 103:14 says, God knows our frame. He remembers what we are like. He is not surprised about these things. Wanting to make sure we're saved is a natural, human response to doubt.

NEED FOR ASSURANCE

As parents, we may not say anything immediately if we hear a child make the statement, "I asked Jesus into my heart again today." Wait for a good teachable moment when the subject comes up naturally and then say, "When we come to Jesus, we're his forever. Nothing can separate us from God's love." We can teach about assurance without making a frontal attack on their repeated prayers for salvation.

Children need reassurance. Parents can move alongside a child and say, "You know, aren't you glad that Jesus will never, ever let you out of his hands? He's never going to let you go. You're part of his family forever; just like you'll always be our child." It's also helpful to memorize biblical promises about assurance, such as John 10:28, with a child. That's where we need to go when doubts come.

DISCIPLESHIP IN THE HOME

Our goal as Christian parents is to lead our children into a personal relationship with the Lord Jesus Christ, then spend the rest of their growing years training them. First we're born into God's family, then the lifelong process of discipleship begins.

It's often hard for a parent to know, though, if a child has sincerely received Jesus Christ as Savior or not. Outward displays of emotion at a point of decision aren't a reliable barometer. Tears are irrelevant to the sincerity of one's commitment. A child's heart attitude is what counts, but that isn't always easy for a parent to discern.

As parents, we often see things in our children's lives that are inconsistent with Christianity. It's in the home where our worst side often comes out. But it's helpful when you're looking at your child and wondering, "Is this kid really a Christian?" to remember our own struggles as young people. We need to have long memories.

Philippians 1:6 says, "I am confident that he who began a good work in you will perfect it until the day of Christ Jesus." As soon as a child accepts Jesus Christ as Savior, he or she is saved. God has begun a good work in that child's life, even if we can't always see it.

TWELVE

Providing the Right Role Models

Carol Smith

I LOVE BEING AROUND ROB AND JAY. A part of a happy family, they are secure and loved. Their parents have placed a priority on loving God, each other, and their boys. Rob is more like his Dad each time I see him. He walks like him and jokes like him. I sat across the dinner table from Rob recently. The night had grown long and he was coming closer and closer to falling asleep at the table. When, at last, Mom sent him toward his bedroom, Rob kissed his Mom and Dad on the cheek as he told us all good night. It was beautiful to see how he has grown into the pattern that loving parents have set.

It was quite different sitting across the table from Todd at McDonald's. Todd's home was a battlefield from the beginning. It was obvious that by age thirteen Todd had not learned a working sense of right and wrong. He had already been treated for chemical dependency and emotional disturbance. "I'm afraid for you," I said. "I'm afraid you think that anything's right as long as you don't get caught."

"Yeah," Todd said, brightening up, "that's what my Dad

said. He said he did all the stuff that I did, but he just didn't get caught.''

Todd and Rob are both walking comfortably in the patterns they have been shown. They are playing the part which comes most naturally. They are following their primary role models—their parents.

Role models are the people who show us how to behave, how to relate. They are the people from whom we learn the part we are to play. They are our mentors in how we *see* ourselves as well as *present* ourselves. What they value, we tend to value. What they cheer, we tend to cheer. If our role models are warm, caring people with the ability to be emotionally intimate in their significant relationships, we have a good chance of becoming healthy, loving adults. We have seen it modeled. We have a pattern to follow. If, on the other hand, our role models are abusive, emotionally unavailable, or physically absent, we can easily follow that pattern even to the point of sickness.

A word of qualification. Each adult has the choice to change, to modify who he is or what habits she has accumulated. Our role models as children do not have control over our adult choices. But as children, we *are* influenced by those who most frequently model for us how to live. The impression is a strong and lasting one.

WHAT AM I DOING?

So what is a parent to do? No parent is perfect. Each parent is a fallen being in a fallen world. Not only that, each parent was reared by a parent who was also fallen. Our ways are not God's ways. But, being and providing good role models doesn't mean being perfect or appearing flawless. There are concrete ways parents can evaluate and improve the roles they model and provide for their children.

1. Be aware of your influence. Be conscious of the responsibility you accepted in bringing a child into the world. Classical pianists face a technical challenge when they play a piece with a melody line buried within arpeggios and counter melodies. The fingers that hit that melody line must play more loudly than all the others even as all the other fingers are playing. An interesting fact is that if the pianist will concentrate on that melody line as she plays, that line will begin to ring above the rest even before the tedious practice hours it will take to solidify the effect. In a similar way if a parent keeps active in her mind that she is modeling for her children how to live life, she will find it easier to evaluate the messages she is sending. She will also catch opportunities and teachable moments that otherwise might get lost in the momentum of the day.

2. Realize children are always learning. Rick is taking his dog to obedience school. What a time they have had. Master and forty-pound pup are feeling the strains of an artificial environment where the clash of the wills is a given. Rick remarked the other day that he had realized that he was constantly teaching Barney. There was never a time when he wasn't consciously or unconsciously reinforcing some behavior—good or bad.

One of the greatest problems Rick has with Barney is the old run-up-and-down-the-fence-and-bark-at-the-neighbor's-dog habit. Rick tried standing in Barney's way, isolating him in his time-out dog house, and yelling "NO" as loudly as possible. Rick has probably tried more than any other average, loving dog owner to peacefully train Barney out of this irritating habit. But, somehow Barney just isn't catching it. "Why is my human being so difficult?" he must think. "Is this some new game?"

Thanks to the gift of a video camera Rick and his wife, Teresa, gained some insight into the habits of their wayward pet. There they all are, on tape, mere months ago, saying, "Here Barney! Come see Bear (the neighbor's dog)! Look at them run together. How cute! Come 'ere Barney! Run with Bear." Rick and Teresa smile sheepishly. Without realizing it, they trained Barney into the very behavior they are now trying to discipline. A baby is expected soon in the same household. What an object lesson Barney will be. Children, even more than pups, are always learning.

3. Practice what you preach. A full-page painting opened an article in *Parents Magazine.* The title of the article was "The Best Kept Secret about Discipline." In the painting, a police officer was using one hand to push a teenager up to the front door of a home. In the other hand the policeman carried a stolen candy bar. The front door was open, showing the father, dripping wet, obviously having been called from the shower to face his shoplifting son. The punch line of the painting was that the towel the father grabbed as a wrap as he scurried from the shower displayed a hotel name in bold letters. We don't need to read the article. We know the best kept secret of discipline just from the opening page. Discipline begins with the parents' behavior.

The first illustration of the article goes something like this. A mother is seen rushing over to her child who has hit a younger child. The mom smacks her son and says, "That'll teach you to not hit someone littler than you!" Get the picture?

I was riding in the car with a youth minister. His son was small enough to ride in a car seat, but we had forgotten it. The son was also big enough to stand in the floorboard of the backseat and lean between the front seats. As we sat at the red light we spotted a policeman approaching from the right. On impulse my friend said, "Brandon, sit down. There's a policeman!" Realizing what he had communicated, he quickly added, "The policeman wants you to be safe."

"Good rescue," I thought to myself.

A few blocks down the road Brandon asked, "Daddy, is the policeman gone?" After an affirmative reply Brandon sighed, "Good! I can stand back up now."

My friend and I exchanged the sideways "uh-oh" glance with the postlude sheepish smile out the window. Now, I know my friend did not want to train his son to hide from policemen. He probably had even expressed to his son that policemen were there to help him. But, Brandon gave a good reminder that not only are children always learning, they hear what is practiced more than what is preached.

4. Practice now the values you hope to see in your kids when they are adults. Try this exercise. Get out a piece of paper and draw a line vertically down the middle so that you have two long columns. In one column make a list of the characteristics or values you would hope to see in your child as an adult. Then, in the other column, rate *yourself* from 1 to 10 on each of those qualities. Let's say that 1 is "I don't see this in myself at *all*" and 10 is "I've got that covered."

How did you do? The bottom line is you can't expect your kids to excel in areas that you don't value. Keep in mind, though, that you *can* expect your children to excel even where you stumble. They can see you fall. They should also see you grieve over and correct your mistakes. That teaches them much more than a perfect score ever will.

5. Model a life that both needs and receives the grace of God. Accept the fact that this world is fallen and you are a part of it. You cannot influence your child in *everything* that is good and worthwhile. There's not the time in a day, nor the energy in a life. But you *can* model a dependence on God and his grace that will provide a secure foundation for your child no matter the specific weaknesses or strengths she might have. There are some traits we all need, and dependence on God is a primary one. Not a perfect life, but rather a life touched by God's grace.

One of the things that has kept our fallen heroes down is

their inability to admit mistakes. It has become more honorable to slink off in the darkness or exploit a failure than to confess and change. This is reflected in the fact that we have begun to honor those who seem not to need at all—the anti-hero. What we really need are role models who are brave enough to let God be the only all-sufficient one. We need role models who will model values of obedience to God, repentance from sin, and grace received. These are values that will help keep kids Christian.

THIRTEEN

Blessing Your Child with Rites of Passage

John Trent

A S WE SKIDDED OUR BICYCLES TO A STOP in front of our house, my twin brother and I both looked up and saw the same thing. There it was. Staring at us with its one pitiless, accusing eye. Without a word being spoken, we both knew that we were in major trouble.

As a child, I hated living on the street corner. It wasn't that our home wasn't nice. It was the fact that living in the corner house meant the street light was planted right in our yard.

"Be home before the street light comes on!" was the iron-clad law we lived under. There was no "fudge factor" allowed in our home. All my grandmother had to do was look out the window and see if we'd made it home before the street light came on . . . and once again we hadn't.

I know that for today's parents, the topic of spanking has become controversial. But when I grew up, there was no controversy. My grandparents were helping my mother raise three sons in a single-parent home, and they believed firmly in spanking. And being home after the street light came on was grounds for the board of education being applied to the seat of knowledge.

Like the condemned taking his last, long walk, I shuffled down the hall to my grandfather's room to receive my spanking. I knew that two swats on the posterior with his old-style razor strap were ahead. But little did I know that one of the greatest times of blessing in my life lay ahead as well.

As I look back today, that evening provided me with a meaningful "rite of passage" from childhood to young adulthood. For years afterward, it shaped my behavior, and directly affected my attitudes and actions. What's more, it gave me one of the clearest pictures I ever had of my grandfather's love for me . . . and his love for Christ.

AN UNEXPECTED BLESSING EVENING

Whenever my brother, Jeff, and I were in trouble at the same time, I always went first to get my spanking. (It was only years later that I found out that my "smart" brother would use those few extra minutes to fill his back pockets with Kleenex to soften the blows.) Two swats and a few tears later, I was back in the kitchen with my grandmother.

"Go get your grandfather for dinner," she said. Not wanting to risk another spanking, I headed down the hallway to knock on my grandfather's door.

Many children grow up calling their grandparents, "Gramps," "Grampie," "Grampa," or some other affectionate nickname; not us. Anytime we addressed him we were to call him "Grandfather" or "Sir." What's more, it was a "two-swat" offense to ever enter his room without politely knocking at the door and waiting for him to beckon us to enter.

I was about to knock on the door when I noticed it was already slightly open. That's why I broke the cardinal rule and gently pushed the door open.

What I saw shocked me. There was my grandfather, a man

who rarely showed any emotion, sitting on the end of his bed crying. I stood at the door in confusion, not knowing what to say. Suddenly, he looked up at me, and I froze where I was. I had no idea what was to come when my grandfather spoke to me.

"Come here, John," he said to me, his voice full of emotion. I walked over to him, fully expecting to be disciplined for not knocking on the door. But instead of a swat, he reached out and took me in his arms. He hugged me closely, and in tears he told me how much he loved each of us boys, and how deeply it hurt him to have to spank us.

"John, I want more than anything in life for each of you to become godly, righteous young men. I've tried my best, but I've made a decision tonight. I'm never going to spank you boys again.

"I've done all I could to see that you know what's right, and that you live your life by God's rules. John, I won't always be here to remind you. *Besides, you're a young man now.* I hope you know how much I love you, how proud I am of each of you, and how much I pray for you. And I hope you'll continue to be the man God wants you to be throughout all your life. . . ."

I can't explain it, but when I left his room that night, I was a different person. It was as if I had traded in the boy for the man. In a way, that night provided a "rite of passage" for me. For the first time, I had received my grandfather's blessing. He knew that I was indeed at an important transition point in my life. I was leaving childhood and entering young adulthood . . . and the decisions I made needed to honor the Lord. He also had an inner knowledge that he didn't have long to live, and he wanted his words of blessing to stay with me.

Three months later, in that same room, my grandfather died instantly and unexpectedly when a blood vessel burst in his brain. I thank God that I didn't make it home before the street light turned on that night three months before. For

I know now that the Lord allowed me to experience a time of blessing with the most important man in my early life.

In an unexpected, unrehearsed way, my grandfather gave me a gift whose effects have stayed with me for a lifetime. What he allowed me to experience is something foreign to our culture, but was common in Old Testament homes.

GIFTS OF GREAT LOVE:
"RITES OF PASSAGE" FOR YOUR CHILDREN

We've lost something in our modern society that for generations was a powerful means of shaping young lives for the Savior. No child who lived in Old Testament times would ever reach adulthood, undertake a long journey, or get married without it. It was an important tool parents used to communicate their love for a child, and their love for God.

What was this "something" that was so important in Old Testament times, and yet is so ignored in our own? It was a specific time when a parent blended loving words and caring actions into a meaningful ceremony designed to leave a lasting memory. In a nutshell, no child could pass the major milestone markers in life without experiencing a "blessing ceremony" from his parents.

Far from being a trite, meaningless ritual; a blessing ceremony often provided a stability point for the rest of a child's life. It was used as a "rite of passage" where encouraging words marked an important transition point in a child's life. Perhaps most of all, it gave a child the tangible knowledge that his parent's blessing, and the Lord's, was with him as he stepped out to face the future.

For the biblical basis for providing children with a "blessing ceremony," one need only turn to Genesis 27. Most of us are so familiar with the story there of Jacob receiving his father's blessing, and his brother Esau missing it, that we turn quickly past these pages. But as parents who desire to leave a loving legacy in a child's life—especially a spiritual one—we will do well to walk slowly and look closely at this powerful Old Testament concept.

Every time Old Testament parents "blessed" their child, several important, life-changing things took place. Each one powerfully incorporated loving words with caring actions in the context of a special evening or event. All of them combined to leave a mark on a child that could shape his life for years to come.

Do you have a child in your home who is nearing an important "milestone marker" in life (entering grade school or high school; going away to college, trade school, or the service; preparing for marriage or the birth of his first child; or even embarking on a new business or career)? *Then why not do what Old Testament parents never failed to do at important transition points in their children's lives.*

Why not design a special evening just for him or her that signals his or her "rite of passage" into another important phase of life? You might begin the evening with a special meal, and then for dessert, serve up loving words and actions into a time of "blessing." As you'll see, even an informal ceremony can give your children strength, courage, and encouragement enough to chew on for a lifetime.

What can make this memorable evening a success? What are these "elements" of the Old Testament blessing? They are the very same things that were a part of my "unexpected" time of blessing with my grandfather. And they remain the same things that can help you to mark your child for Christ today. While Gary Smalley and I go into them in detail in our book *The Blessing,* in a nutshell these important elements are:

1. Meaningful touching. Isaac says to his son, Jacob, "Come close and kiss me, my son" (Gn 27:26). Jacob says of his grandchildren, "Bring them to me, please, that I may bless them . . . and he kissed them and embraced them . . ." (Gn

48:9-10). It even says that when Jesus called the children to him, "He took them in his arms and began blessing them, laying his hands upon them" (Mk 10:16).

For a child, things become real when he is touched. Just go to Disneyland and watch a two-year-old meet Mickey Mouse. Once they get over their initial fear, children will almost all reach out and touch the costume character... and the look in their eyes says it all. Mickey or Minnie has come off the TV screen and into real life.

That night with my grandfather, as much as anything, it was his strong arms gently hugging me that told me I had received his blessing. As he sat next to me on the bed with his arm around my shoulder, his desire for me to live a godly life and words of blessing took on ten times their weight in my mind.

2. Spoken Message. Do you know the very first thing the Lord did after he created man and woman? "God blessed them..." (Gn 1:28). God has always been one to bless others through the "spoken" word. He "spoke" and the whole world came into being (1:3ff). It was his "word" that came to Abraham and guaranteed that all his offspring would one day be blessed with a Savior (12:1-3). And it was his "Word that became flesh and dwelt among us..." (Jn 1:14). In both the Old and New Testaments, there was never a "blessing" that wasn't verbalized.

What does this say to parents today? Namely, we can't hide behind the words, *"They know I love them without me having to tell them...."* Most children who are left to fill in the blanks when it comes to hearing loving words from their parents aren't really sure they're loved at all. At the very least, they certainly haven't received what the Bible calls a blessing.

For a child today—especially one standing at an important transition point in life—spoken words of blessing can be tremendously important. They were for me.

Even though I knew it deep inside, I had never heard my grandfather say, "I love you" before that night. But once the words were out, my love for him *and desire to live up to his expectations of me* tripled on the spot. Some parents even write down a special blessing for their son or daughter at a blessing evening. But whether our words are written on paper or simply on the tablets of their hearts, hearing words of blessing brings life, strength, and confidence to our children's hearts (Prv 18:21).

But what words? If we're to follow the biblical pattern, they will be words that picture a special future for the child being blessed.

3. Picturing a special future. Steve Lyon, a very valuable staff member at our ministry, shared an important time of blessing he experienced with his parents. They spent only a few minutes and two dollars on a milk shake to create the event; but what took place has stayed with him for a lifetime.

At the time it happened, Steve was like most sixth graders on their way into the unknown world of junior high school—nervous. He knew those years were going to be full of challenges and excitement: managing his own locker, walking from class to class, making his way through wood shop, gym class, and going through puberty.

The first night of school, seventh graders and their parents were invited to an open house at the school. Steve and his parents came to the evening's activities, and on their way home his father took an unexpected turn into a neighborhood shopping center. Parking his car in front of Steve's favorite ice cream parlor, his father led the three of them to a table where they each ordered their favorite dessert.

They were there only twenty minutes. But in those twenty minutes his parents provided him with words of blessing and hope that still encourage him twenty years later.

"Son, we're proud of you," they said. "You're growing up

into a man so fast. What's more, we know you're going to do very well here. And we know you'll make us proud of you. . . ."

Married now, with a child of his own, Steve recently told me, "That was one of the most important days of my life. My parents may not have realized it at the time, but they blessed me by creating one of the most special memories of my life. Their words gave me the certainty that with God and their blessing, I would do well in junior high, and in the future. I'd never gone out with just them before; and when we did, it turned my fear of the future into eager anticipation."

On the night of his betrayal, Jesus went to great lengths to assure the timid disciples that they had a special future with him. (Jn 13:1ff). If only parents realized how powerful their words of blessing can be for a child (or young adult) facing a fork in life's road that hides an unknown future.

"SON OF OUR FATHER"

In certain African tribes today, when a young boy reaches the age of manhood (considered between twelve and fourteen), he goes through a very special ceremony. For years he will look forward to this evening. Then, unexpectedly one night, the boy is suddenly awakened by the loud shouts of men outside his hut.

The boy's father, along with all the other men of the village, is standing outside. Each man is painted up like a warrior, and each beats the ends of his spear on the ground chanting, "Come out, *son*. . . . Come out, *son*. . . ."

For this boy, the ceremony is a picture of his being "called out" from boyhood and into manhood. He races out of his hut, away from his mother and outside to where the men stand. Then his father and the chief of the tribe will lay their hands on him and say, "You are now *the son of my people*."

That night with my grandfather, I knew that I was being

called out to become a *"son of my Heavenly Father."* I had reached a major transition point in my life, and his words and meaningful touch encouraged me in the right direction.

We know of parents who have designed a special "blessing" ceremony for their daughter entering grade school and for a son going away to one of our service academies. We once sat through a beautiful, emotional time of blessing as both sets of parents used a "butterfly" motif at a rehearsal dinner to give a blessing to their children who would marry the next day. In each case, this special, focused time of love and encouragement profoundly affected not only the children . . . but the entire family.

I'm not advocating the return to meaningless rituals or contrived ceremonies. But what I am challenging us all to consider—especially those of us who are parents—is to provide a focused time when our loving words and caring touch can "call out" our children to serve their Heavenly Father.

Part 4

Shaping Children

FOURTEEN

Praying with and for Your Children

Susan Yates

THE KITCHEN DOOR SLAMMED shut, and the basketball landed with a thud on the linoleum floor. Glancing up from the pile of dishes, I came face-to-face with a twelve-year-old ready to explode with frustration. His red face and clinched fists only exaggerated the fuse that was about to blow.

"Hey, John, what's up?" I asked, trying to play the cool Mom.

"Todd makes me sooo angry," erupted my steamed-up son. "He always acts like he's the greatest basketball player in the world and he makes me feel like I'm the worst."

"How does he do that?" I inquired.

"I went for a lay-up and he said, 'That was a dumb shot.' Then I missed a pass and he said, 'Can't you even catch it?' He's always saying how good he is and showing off. Just because he's thirteen, he thinks he's the greatest. He's mean to everyone. I'm never going to play with him again."

Laying aside the dirty spaghetti pot, I put my arms around my son. His macho determination dissolved just a little and I noticed a tear quickly brushed away. As I hugged him I silently cried out to God, "What do I do now?"

This was not the first time Todd had been the source of unhappiness in the neighborhood. My younger son had also been the victim of Todd's putdowns. How should I respond?

FACING GOD TOGETHER

This was not a four-year-old with a skinned knee. A bandaid and hugs would not alleviate this pain. As I struggled with my response, I thought about my renewed desire for our family to grow in our prayer life. Perhaps I should pray with John.

But Lord, I found myself thinking, *I don't even know how to pray. I'd like to pound Todd myself. And besides, what if I pray with John and it doesn't help? Then my son's faith will be damaged. It was easier to pray with the children when they were younger and problems weren't so complex. Then I could control it more. It's scary now.*

Through my jumbled emotions I began to realize that this was an opportunity to come to God together with my son. I did not have the answer. I needed God just as much as John did. I could not fix this situation. We would have to lean on the Lord together.

"Son," I said, "I don't know what to do. I'm angry with Todd too, but what we have to do is to pray for God to help us. He will teach us something special through this hard situation."

Together we simply prayed for God's help. We prayed for God to help Todd during this awkward teenage season and to bring him through this time of putting younger kids down. Then we prayed for John's behavior not to be dictated by Todd's hurtful ways, but instead for God to help him respond in a loving way and compliment Todd's basketball shots.

It wasn't the end of the unpleasant experience. Several more times we had to pray for Todd. And yet there was much that John and I learned. I learned that, as our children grow older, it will not be as easy for us to fix a situation or come up with a ready answer. While initially frustrating, this is actually a blessing. We are forced to go to the Lord with our child and to rely solely on him for the solution. This gives us a sense of equal partnership with our child in approaching God with a need.

My son was learning that his parents couldn't fix everything. More and more he would need *to look to God for guidance.*

COMMON FEARS

Our experience with Todd exemplified one of several fears that we as Christians face as we attempt to pray with and for our children. I feared my inability to handle the situation in a manner that would encourage spiritual growth. But I learned that there is great freedom in not having an answer and that peace comes and faith grows as we pray to God honestly about our needs.

A second fear parents often experience is: *What if God doesn't answer? Won't my child's faith be damaged?* I've learned children are helped when they recognize that God answers prayer in three ways: "No," "Yes," and "Wait." (Like parents!) But God always answers out of love. There may be a long silence with the "wait," which we find difficult. Yet we must remember that God is not bound by our timetables. He does what is best, not necessarily what is fast. God is not limited to our resources. His ways are far better than ours.

When God answers a prayer "no," it is especially important to be reminded that his "no" is a "love no." If your three-year-old wanted to play ball in the street, you would probably say "no" because, in your wisdom, you know that it would be dangerous. If your sixteen-year-old wanted to get married, you'd likely say wait. Again your response is motivated by love. When your child asks for forgiveness, you will say yes. Recognizing how God answers prayer enables us to go to him in honesty and without fear.

A third fear we might experience is that our own lack of spiritual knowledge and maturity will hinder the work of God in the lives of our children. It is easy to look at another believer who seems so mature and wonder if God doesn't answer more of her prayers than he does ours because she is more mature. Or we look at our own lives and we see much that is not right and we wonder how we can teach our children to obey God when we ourselves fall so far short.

God is far more interested in our desire to grow than in our "level of maturity." We will never become "mature" in Christ this side of heaven and what our Father desires is a heart that is continuously seeking to be obedient. He does not expect us to have *all* the answers. He alone does. He knows that we will fail. His forgiveness does not run out. We go to God in prayer not because of who *we* are but because of who *he* is.

PRAYING FOR OUR CHILDREN

When we pray for our children we need to be reminded that these children really belong to God. They are on loan to us for a short time. He loves them even more than we do and desires that they grow in faith. He knows what their needs are and what the future holds for them.

The first principle in praying for our children simply involves asking God for sharp antennae. Antennae receive signals that are around us but can't be seen without the right equipment. As parents we need sharp antennae that can discern the subtle needs of our children.

Regularly, I pray, "God, give me sharp antennae so I can pick up needs in the life of this child."

Perhaps a small child needs an extra dose of appreciation

for his attempts at bed-making. Maybe a teenager needs some "space" today and not a long list of parental reminders. As we ask, God will fine-tune our antennae.

Second, it is helpful to take some time at least once a year to discuss with our mates the needs of each child in five basic areas: spiritual, mental, emotional, social, and physical. When we discern these needs we become aware of some actions that can be taken. We also become aware of how to pray specifically for each child.

Perhaps our young child is beset by bedtime fears. An emotional need is for God to give this child peace at bedtime. When we experienced this with our twins, we shared Psalm 121 with them and we told them that we would check on them every twenty minutes or so after they went to bed. Over a period of time and much prayer, we have seen God bring peace in this area.

A physical need might be for better eating habits. Breakfast time can be difficult with the predominance of junk cereals on the market. A friend of mine with three boys solved this dilemma by having a weekend cereal shelf. During the weekdays the boys ate healthy breakfasts, but on the weekends they were permitted junk cereals. Sometimes in meeting needs we must pray for creative ideas or creative friends with ideas!

My husband, Johnny, and I have found it helpful to get away by ourselves for a couple of days every August. We take time to think through each of our five children in these five areas for the coming year. We write down the needs we see and discuss them together. The resulting lists of needs become the basis of our daily prayers for each child for the coming year. I am with the children more than my husband is, but I am encouraged to know that he is aware of and praying for the specific needs of each child. It is wonderful at the end of the year to look back and to see how God has answered our prayers.

We also have a list of different character traits that we are praying each of our children will develop. A heart of compassion, a teachable spirit, and a deep sense of integrity are three of those on our list. It is beneficial to discuss with your mate the traits that are important to your family.

To avoid being overwhelmed by all of the prayer needs, I have a prayer notebook in which I write down specific things I pray for each day. Every day I am praying for my immediate family in different areas of need. In addition I pray one day for friends in other parts of the country, another for marriages, another for the needs of our church, and so on. Simple organization keeps me from being overwhelmed.

Enlisting other adults to pray for our children is another important principle. If your child has godparents, let them know specific things to be praying for their godchild. Enlist grandparents to pray. Recently I asked my eighty-two-year-old mother-in-law if she was praying for my children's mates. She is, and I hope some future in-laws somewhere are praying for my children and for us as we raise them.

For the past five years I have met weekly with a group of women to pray for the public schools that our children attend. We pray for the teachers, for the staff, and for our kids. Often we pray for our children to get caught if they are doing anything that they should not be doing! Recently one of the children was caught helping a friend with a quiz. This became a valuable growing experience for both the child and her parents.

As we pray for our children, we will be forced to look to God to meet their needs. The older our kids get, the more we will grow in recognizing our tremendous need to be in prayer for them.

PRAYING WITH OUR CHILDREN

One of the greatest blessings of praying with our children is that the act of praying together serves as a reminder to us that parent and child are equal in their need for God. This acceptance enables us to live lives of honesty rather than pretense. A Christian home is not a place where perfect parents live. Rather it is a home where parent and child alike are growing in their relationships with Christ. This is a lifelong process from which there is no graduation. When we are on our knees with our child we are humbled.

Helping our small children learn about the character of God sets the tone for prayer times together. There are five "always"—one for each finger—which we use to describe God. He is always there, always answers, always understands, always forgives, and always loves. Considering these five qualities of God gives us confidence to go to him in prayer.

Our attitude in prayer should be one of honesty and naturalness, yet we often feel awkward. Any new relationship is by nature awkward. There is a "getting to know one another" that is initially uncomfortable. At different ages, awkwardness will intensify. Small children can be a real encouragement in overcoming awkwardness because they are instinctively natural and honest. Our daughter Allison at a young age once prayed: "Dear Lord, please help the babysitters to be able to handle us!" That was a very real prayer in our family!

But what do we do if our child does not want to pray? Relax. There have been times in each of our lives when we have been the silent one too. If a child does not want to pray, simply help her think of something she would like you to pray for her during the prayer time, and remember her request. Our children need not pray, but they must be quiet while others do. This is politeness to family members and basic respect for God. We have found that usually out of our gang of five kids, there is at least one who is more inclined to pray than another. Sometimes different stages in development cause a child to be more private or more open. It is important to respect those times, and not to push.

A vital home will be one in which prayer takes place both

spontaneously and in a planned setting. Planned prayer times are likely to be at meal times and bedtime. A special family night also provides time for planned prayer. Beside our breakfast table is a huge bulletin board with pictures falling off in every direction. Each picture is of a friend who lives out of town. Every morning at breakfast a different family member gets to choose someone to pray for from the board. During the Christmas season we take turns drawing one of the new Christmas cards out of a basket, and the leader for the day prays for that family. From time to time, we have also kept a prayer notebook by our table. In it we jot down special concerns for which we are praying and then how God answers them. Recently we were praying for a new friend for our cousin Thomas who had moved to a new school. Last week we were able to write Patrick down as an answer to our prayer. Planned prayer times promote a sense of stability and security.

Spontaneous prayers reveal the vitality of our faith. These are prayers that are offered up throughout the day in response to immediate circumstances. This week my twin ten-year-olds came in from school feeling very distressed. They are patrols on the school bus and had had a difficult time with the bus driver. As they shared their story with me I said, "Gals, why don't we pray right now for this driver." Susy and Libby did, and we were encouraged.

Recently I was leaving for a speaking engagement about which I was very nervous. Just before leaving, I was chatting with my son, Chris. When he asked me about my talk I told him I was nervous and asked him to pray for me then. He did, and I was comforted. It is wonderful to have a Heavenly Father to whom we can take our immediate concerns. Too often we think, "I will pray about that later." And then we forget. Enthusiasm for our faith will grow as we learn to pray spontaneously.

The most frequently needed spontaneous prayer is the request for forgiveness. One day, after lashing out at one of my girls, I realized that the problem was not hers but mine. I was tired and I had acted unfairly. I needed to ask her forgiveness, so I went to her room and said, "Libby, I was wrong, I should not have said what I did. I would like you to forgive me. Will you forgive me?" She said yes. As we prayed together, I also asked God to forgive me, and he did. Forgiveness is the most important ingredient in the home.

Integrating the Word of God into our prayer times will enable us to experience not only the supernatural power of God but also his practical nature. It has been said that there are over three thousand promises in the New Testament alone for us to claim. Growing in Christ involves taking God up on his promises. As we learn to let God's word guide our prayer, we can also teach our children to pray this way.

Allison, our oldest, is a high school senior struggling with college decisions. The promise in Scripture which we are praying is, "If any of you lack wisdom, let him ask of God who gives to all men generously" (Jas 1:5). I don't think any one of the seven of us will ever forget that promise. We can't wait to see how God answers! As our children learn to mix their prayers with God's promises, they will begin to trust in the relevancy of his word.

BENEFITS OF PRAYER

I was blessed to grow up in a strong Christian home and to marry into one as well. Before we got married we read many books on how to have a good marriage. Before we had children we did the same thing. Surely, I remember thinking, raising a family can't be that difficult! And then I had three kids. And then we had twins! Suddenly all of my expectations of what it would be like to raise a family dissolved. Used to a successful career, I now found myself failing miserably in being the mother I had assumed I could be. Finally, one night in tears I prayed, "Lord, I can't do it.

I'm a failure and that is all I can offer you—not success but small victories and lots of failures.'' God began to remind me that he knew that, and that he simply wanted me with all of my failures. After all, these were his kids, and my confidence needed to be in him rather than in my own ability.

When we are on our knees, our focus shifts from ourselves back to God. In praying for our children, we are reminded over and over that they are indeed his kids and that we must trust him for their spiritual development. We must allow him the privilege of working in their lives differently than he has in ours.

When we see God answer our children's prayers, our faith will grow. When we do not know how to fix things for them, he will show the way. When we pray with them, we are weaning them from relying on parents who will not always be with them to dependence upon their Heavenly Father who will never leave them.

FIFTEEN

Growing Tender Children in a Tough World

Pat Palau

WHEN OUR CHILDREN WERE SMALL, I used to say to them, teasingly, "It's more blessed to give than to receive, isn't it?" They would reply, "No, it isn't ... getting is better!"

Learning to care is a spiritual discipline that requires constant nurturing. Our responsibility as parents is to help our children to become tender toward the less fortunate, especially those who still don't know the Lord Jesus Christ as Savior.

Not long ago I had the joy of visiting with a good friend from university days. Diane has served for twenty-seven years as a teacher of missionary children at Faith Academy in the Philippines. Because she's worked with children for so long, I asked her, "What kind of children do we have nowadays?"

Diane replied, "We have a lot of great teaching now for parents on building a child's self-esteem. Even five-year-olds are more confident than they used to be. But there's a flip side to it. Children have also become more selfish."

The Bible tells us that we are special. Our children need to hear that. But that's not all. We also need to care about other people and learn to put them first, just as Jesus Christ did.

Here are seven strategies that my husband Luis and I have found effective for raising tenderhearted children.

1. Sponsor a child, especially a needy boy or girl living in a Third World country. When Luis and I first thought about sponsoring a child years ago, we discussed it with our sons and suggested "adopting" a boy from Mexico. They thought that was a great idea since we used to live there. Since then, we've sponsored children through several organizations. One we highly recommend is Compassion International (P.O. Box 7000, Colorado Springs, Colorado 80933).

Several years ago Luis took our youngest son, Stephen, with him to a youth conference where Luis was speaking. While there, Stephen saw a presentation on sponsoring children. He was so touched that he brought home a picture of an orphan, promising to support this little boy forever. I've helped out, and today he still supports that child. Be willing to pitch in if your child shows a sensitivity and desire to share.

2. Encourage your children to watch the news on television and read your daily newspaper or a national news magazine. Learning about cities or nations affected by natural disasters and hearing about other tragedies is important. We live in a real world. After discussing current events, cross over to discuss what God is doing in those parts of the world.

It's easy to shut our minds off to the needs of the world by saying, "Well, they've lived like that all their lives. They're used to it. They don't notice how bad things really are." But suffering is suffering. Every parent and child, no matter where he lives, feels pain the same way we do.

3. Inform your children about the world's major religions. Becoming tenderhearted involves understanding that the religions of the world inevitably enslave people and often make their lives miserable. Helping children to see that most people are under the domination of Satan won't make them feel superior or arrogant, especially if parents have displayed respect and genuine love for people from all walks of life. By word and example we can communicate to our children that "we don't ridicule or make fun of people, even in private."

4. Have an encyclopedia and globe handy. Utilize these resources to look things up with your children. Another excellent resource is *Operation World* by Patrick Johnstone (Multnomah Press). This book combines facts and figures about the peoples, populations, economies, politics, and religions of the world from a Christian perspective. It also includes helpful maps and graphs.

5. Become active in your local church missions program. Invite missionaries into your home and let your children take part in dinner table conversations. This is one of the best ways to get to know some of God's servants. When I was growing up we had many missionaries in our home. By talking about different people and customs, they made other parts of the world seem more real to me.

6. Read missionary biographies with your children. *From Jerusalem to Irian Jaya* by Ruth Tucker (Zondervan) has brief segments about scores of Christian missionaries. Both children and parents will find the stories exciting. Biographies for youth on the lives of William Carey, Mary Slessor, Hudson Taylor, and other great missionaries also are available.

Children especially enjoy hearing about George Müller, whose specialty was trusting God to what some might call an extreme. He took in thousands of orphans from the streets of England and cared for them, providing the best of everything without asking anyone but God for financial help.

There were several times when Müller's family would be without food, but they would set the table anyway as if they were awaiting a meal. Once a cart laden with bread broke down in the street right outside their home. The bread man came to their door saying, "I don't know what to do with all this bread because I can't take it any further. Could you use it?" The lesson the orphans learned was to look to God for everything—a good lesson for us today.

7. Deliberately forgo something in order to emphasize giving to others. "Live simply so that others might simply live." Let your children see how what you have given up has helped others. They may think of other things they don't need either.

As missionaries, we've been on the receiving end of other children's generosity. One group of children saved their money all summer while we were living overseas so that they could buy our sons a bicycle. That gift really meant a lot to us.

Several years ago after moving back to the United States, our family discussed whether to install a deck and hot tub in our backyard or use that same amount of money to take our sons with us to visit several countries. We mutually decided that our money would be better spent traveling together. Involving our sons in that decision made visiting other mission fields that much more significant.

It isn't easy to cultivate spiritual tenderness in the heart of a child, but it's worth the effort. We live in an increasingly cynical, calloused society which affects all of us to some degree. Why should we feel embarrassed if our children cry over the sufferings of others? Instead, we should rejoice to see them growing in their care and concern for others.

We must allow our hearts to be broken by the things that break God's heart. Because he indwells us and desires to work through us, we can become part of the answer to this world's most urgent problems.

Together with your children, discover anew that true happiness and joy are found as the Apostle Paul says, in not looking "only to one's own interests, but also to the interests of others."

SIXTEEN

Teaching Kids to Give

Eddy Hall

"DAD, CAN YOU GET MY JESUS BANK FOR ME?" It was Saturday morning and I had just given five-year-old Jonathan his weekly twenty-five-cent allowance.

"Get mine, too," Janelle called. While I went to get their Jesus banks off the refrigerator, the kids got their piggy banks down from the fireplace mantel. Then with her two banks side by side on the coffee table, Janelle dropped three pennies into her Jesus bank, and her other seven cents into her piggy bank.

"I'm putting a nickel into my Jesus bank every week," Jonathan announced. "Dad, can you help me count my Jesus money?"

For the next few minutes we counted pennies, nickels, dimes, and quarters. "Wow!" Jonathan's eyes got big. "Jesus is rich! A dollar and twenty-eight cents!"

Janelle, three, seemed less impressed with how much money was in her Jesus bank than she was with the urgency of remembering to give to Jesus every week. "If we don't give Jesus money, then he will be hungry," she explained with a look of deep concern, "and that will make him very sad."

From time to time, money comes out of the kids' Jesus

121

banks, and those times can be special. Last Christmas we started a family tradition of having a birthday party for Jesus shortly before Christmas. As we sat around the table after supper I asked the kids, "What shall we give Jesus for a birthday present? Do you know how we can give a present to Jesus?"

"No," they answered.

"Well, Jesus said that any time we help someone who is hungry, or thirsty, or sick, or needs clothes, or is in jail, we are helping him. So what would be some ways we might give Jesus a present?"

We came up with three or four options. The kids chose an idea suggested by my sister—helping the kids in a Central American refugee family come to the United States with their mother to join their father. Jonathan and Janelle emptied their Jesus banks, coming up with a total of thirty-seven cents. Melody and I added some from our sharing fund (our equivalent of their Jesus banks), and they wrapped the gift. Jonathan copied "HAPPY BIRTHDAY, JESUS!" onto the nametag.

Then we all piled into the car to go see the man who was arranging for the plane tickets. The kids presented the gift to him, we lit the candles on the birthday cake we had brought, and everyone sang ". . . happy birthday, dear Jesus!"

Jonathan and Janelle have already forgotten most of the Christmas gifts they gave and received last Christmas, but one gift they still remember clearly: a thirty-seven-cent birthday gift to Jesus.

For our family, Jesus banks are proving to be a great way to nurture both cheerful generosity and responsible steward-ship. Whenever our children get money, they give Jesus his part first. Jesus' part seldom turns out to be less than twenty percent; sometimes it's as much as forty. And giving to Jesus is fun. They love it!

Besides generosity, Jesus banks help our children develop responsibility. Jonathan and Janelle are each responsible to decide how to distribute their Jesus money. Some of it, of course, goes into the offerings at Sunday School and church. Twice, in response to seeing Ethiopian famine victims on TV, Jonathan has sent money from his Jesus bank to a Christian relief organization to help feed hungry people. And sometimes they have a chance to give directly to an individual. They are learning that these are all ways to give to Jesus, and that it is their responsibility to decide how best to help people with their Jesus money.

They are discovering yet one more thing: by setting aside money every week for Jesus, when they learn of a need, they have more to give. Jonathan's last gift for Ethiopia was $1.25. For him, that's five weeks' income! And he still had some left in his Jesus bank for other needs.

The most important way we teach our children about giving is through example. Because much of our family giving consists of giving something tangible to families or individuals, our children are much more aware of our giving than they would be if we only wrote checks. They often go with us to buy a gift or to deliver it. Sometimes one of them even comes up with the idea.

Jonathan is also starting to learn why we don't give to some people or organizations. A few days ago the mail brought a fund raiser letter.

"What is that?" he asked.

"A group wants us to send them money to help with their work."

"Are you going to send them some?"

"No."

"Why not?"

"We're not too crazy about the kinds of things they do."

"Oh. What do they do?"

"Well, they try to help poor people—and that's good—but they put most of their time and money into running programs and don't do much to get to know the people as friends and love them, even though they say that's what's most important to them. We also get tired of them asking for money so often, and that makes us not feel good about giving to them."

"Oh," he said, satisfied, and ran off to play.

For several years Melody and I have found creative giving to be a consistent source of joy in our own lives. We are now discovering that passing that joy along to our children is for us one of the most delightful privileges of being parents.

Part 5

Shaping Teens

SEVENTEEN

What Youth Want from Their Parents

Richard R. and Teresa Dunn

"MARGARET, I AM ALMOST TO THE POINT of giving up on Laura. I have loved her and given to her without asking anything in return for the past seventeen years. But the last six months have been about as much as I can take."

"Helen, I know things have been tough between you two. Has it gotten worse lately?"

"Yes and no. It has seemed worse the past few weeks, but it is actually the same problem as always. Laura and I will be talking together, enjoying the type of mother-daughter relationship I always hoped we would have and then, in only a matter of minutes, we will be at each other's throats. She starts yelling, telling me I don't understand and that I never will. How can I understand her when she won't explain to me what is going on with her?"

"I can relate to having your own child accuse you of being incompetent in the area of understanding. Paul got his driver's license two months ago. I was looking forward to his being able to drive himself to baseball and soccer practice. If only I had known then what I know now."

"What do you mean, Margaret?"

"Ever since he got what he calls his 'ticket to freedom,' our house has been a huge battleground over curfews, gas money, and his use of the car. I am convinced that he received some type of pamphlet with his license which has confirmed his suspicion that I, along with all parents, am indeed completely ignorant."

"Well, Laura must have received that same pamphlet! She asked me to help her pick out a prom dress. As we went shopping I was thinking what a great bond-building time it was going to be for us. Instead, she ridiculed every suggestion I made, pointing out that I was totally out of touch with current fashion. If I am so lacking in contemporary tastes then why did she ask me to go with her in the first place?"

" 'Why?' seems to be the question of the hour, Helen. Do you think we will ever understand what they want from us?"

"Perhaps, but by then they will probably no longer be teenagers."

Adolescents send mixed messages to their parents. Many of their behaviors and statements seem to say to parents, "I want you to be involved in my life. I need to know that your advice and help are always there with me." A few moments later, however, they appear to be communicating, "I want you to give me room to be on my own. I need the freedom to live a life that does not depend on your involvement." Adolescents thus convey a desire for the security of parental support while also implicitly demanding an autonomous relationship to ensure that parents will not get in the way.

Helen is experiencing the frustration of such apparently contradictory signals in her relationship with her daughter, Laura. Margaret has similar feelings as Paul draws her into a series of conflicts over just how much freedom he should be allowed to experience with his new driving privileges. What *do* these adolescents want from their parents? And how can parents respond consistently when what adolescents want seems to change on a daily, even hourly basis?

WHAT ADOLESCENTS REALLY WANT

The confusion begins with the adolescent. Laura and Paul are inconsistent primarily because they are themselves uncertain about how they want their parents to relate to them. Laura probably could not explain exactly why she became so angry with her Mom while they were shopping. All she can identify for herself is that "Mom just does not understand." Paul would be hard-pressed to explain why the rules should be different concerning the use of the car. The point is, "They just don't trust me."

Adolescents are largely unconscious of why they respond erratically, because they are struggling to pass from childhood to adulthood. They react strongly to anything which makes them feel like they are being treated as immature children. Their reactions may include withdrawal, outbursts of anger, or rebellious actions. At the same time, they are not prepared to be adults. They want to act like adults and have adult privileges, but they do not yet have the life experiences and personal resources required for truly being on their own. They become insecure and inhibited when they feel that they must face life without the support of significant adults, especially as it is expressed in loving parental relationships. Thus they look to mom and/or dad to be a secure place of support and approval while also trying to maintain a lifestyle which states boldly, "I am no longer a child."

While the adolescent is experiencing this "push/pull" conflict within, parents are trying to learn how to respond to the adolescent's expression of these attitudes. They become confused as to how to parent their son or daughter who at one moment seems very close and at another, very far away.

There are five common misconceptions which develop as a result of these mixed messages.

1. Relationships with parents and significant adults have become obsolete for an adolescent. Much has been written about the extent to which adolescents are influenced by peer pressure. Certainly this is an age in which one's peers function as the most immediate source of feedback as to how you are doing in life and where you fit in the world. Youth culture and adolescent peers replace parents as the authoritative source for what is fashionable, cool, and acceptable.

Polls taken among adolescents reveal that peers are considered by them to be the number-one influence in their lives. "Friends" are the most important agenda on the student's mind as he or she thinks about his or her social lives. As a result, parents may begin to feel that their adolescent views them and all adults as superfluous.

Yet, while students concentrate their relational energy on their peers, it is their relationships with their parents and other significant adults which has the most permanent influence on the person they are becoming. Note the distinction which has been presented thus far. Peers are the most *immediate* influence, parents are the most *important.*

2. Youth do not really listen to or care about what parents have to say. "How many times have I told you..." is one of those opening phrases parents use during times of exasperation. Parents become convinced that it really does not matter to their adolescent what they say. The youth appears to be disinterested, unaffected, even bored by the entire attempt to communicate. A roll of the eyes, an exaggerated folding of the arms, and a heavy sigh are a few of the nonverbal indicators adolescents use to let the parent know that he is being tuned out like an undesirable radio station.

In fact, students are not only greatly affected by what parents say but also how this is communicated. Adolescents internalize both the verbal and nonverbal messages they receive from parents. Many adults have vivid recall of statements or looks they received from parents when they were teenagers. Nothing goes to the heart of an adolescent as quickly as honest expressions of affirmation like, "I love you and want to understand. Will you help me?" or genuine statements of condemnation like, "You can't do anything right" or "I don't care what you think."

3. Adolescents seek maximum interpersonal distance from parents. This misconception is perhaps a derivative of the first two. Adolescents appear aloof, with no noticeable desire to interact with their parents on a personal level. Parents begin to feel like their adolescent's spending time with them individually or with the family as a whole rates alongside being punished with an after school detention.

Adolescent behavior can reinforce these feelings in a variety of ways. You accompany your son to a school concert or athletic event because you want to be involved in his world. Yet, as soon as you walk in the door of the building, he immediately deserts you to go stand with his friends whom he has been with all day. (At least there are a number of other parents who have been "dumped" with whom you can visit.) You may begin to feel that the most embarrassing event your son could imagine is being seen in public with you!

Yet adolescents are deeply hurt by parents who have no time for them. They translate the word "time" into the word "love." "A parent who cares," they reason, "will be there for me." Adolescents know whose parents attend school functions and whose do not. They also know whose parents are never home and whose are always there to welcome them and their friends. There is an unspoken record of whose parents care enough to take the time to be available.

4. Adolescents would be happiest with complete freedom from their parents. "Maybe I should just give up and let them do what they want to do. At least we would have some peace around here." When surveying the time, energy, and emotional expenditure involved in nurturing and guiding adolescents, it becomes quite tempting for parents to "drop back and punt." Parents become weary of being perceived as the "bad guy," the *only* parent with such demanding and unreasonable expectations, or the old-fashioned, living-in-the-past spoiler of modern social life.

A parent who fails to provide boundaries, however, is one who fails to provide security. Adolescents constantly push against those boundaries, apparently to prove that parents really do not know what they are talking about or do not mean what they say. Yet the worst possible scenario is for them to succeed in removing those boundaries and achieve complete freedom from their parents' influence. For an adolescent, absolute autonomy is equated with isolation.

5. Adolescent sophistication is equivalent to maturity. Contemporary adolescents are living in an information age. They are constantly receiving messages concerning everything from the importance of safe sex to the state of the economy, from the perils of drug abuse to the irreversible effects of a nuclear war. Many adolescents are computer literate, and many are street-smart.

In addition, the contemporary culture has placed adult expectations upon them in areas of employment, education, and social relationships. The combination of these factors has produced a generation of adolescents who appear socially adept and technologically intelligent. They often convey an image of comfort, knowledge, and sophistication.

What is important for parents to understand is that adolescents who imitate adult behaviors, engage in adult conversations, and present a very mature image of confidence are still *adolescents*. In other words, their thoughts, feelings, fears, and needs are still those of a person who is not yet an adult. The failure of adults to help adolescents mature as persons who are not children, yet not quite adults, has led to the problem of many of our youth living with the same stresses as their parents. They cannot take needed time and energy to mature themselves, because they feel the pressure to "act mature" now in order to cope.

PARENTAL RESPONSES TO ADOLESCENT WANTS

Parents can get beyond these misconceptions and respond to the wants of their adolescents by actively responding to the needs which have created those wants. Rather than merely reacting to the daily "push/pull" of adolescents, parents can actively provide consistency which will nurture the students in their faith, personal identity, and ability to relate with others.

1. Provide your adolescent with a secure world of significant adult relationships. Adolescents need parenting and significant interaction with supportive adults, in order to become secure adults themselves. Secure relationships in the home are the primary environment for significant adult relationships. Sponsoring adults such as youth pastors, campus ministry leaders, teachers, coaches, pastors, and family friends provide the necessary adult relationships that allow adolescents to experience independence from parents.

Some specific ways to provide these relationships for your adolescent include:

Love your spouse. From the time he is able to understand the family, a child's greatest desire is that his family love each other. Fathers and mothers need to covenant before God not only to remain married, but also committed to loving one another and having that love permeate the home.

If divorce has already occurred, parents should be careful never to allow the child or adolescent to feel the need to choose between them. The adolescent needs to know he is loved by both parents and feel the freedom to love both without guilt.

Assist them in finding significant adults to serve as role models and disciplers in the faith. Each year movie theaters present an avalanche of movies designed to attract the expendable income of adolescents. In the majority of those movies, the adults are portrayed as inept, preoccupied, and lacking in credibility. The message is clear: teenagers cannot depend on adults. Simply add to this the daily media accounts of the moral failures of civic and religious leaders and it is easy to understand why this generation of adolescents has developed a general mistrust of adults.

The truth is that parents need adults who can be trusted to be present in their adolescents' lives. Because adolescents require a growing independence from parents, they need other significant adults to turn to for wisdom, support, and godly examples. These adults are not substitutes for parents. Rather they are the essential complimentary components for a secure adult world in which adolescents can learn what it means to become a Christian adult.

2. Prioritize positive communication with your adolescent. "Earn the right to be heard." This is a concept essential for parents of an adolescent. From an adult perspective, more than a dozen years of loving care supplied since birth would be sufficient to have earned the right to have your adolescent listen to what you say. But an adolescent views the world differently. Even parents need to work at developing their level of communication with their teenagers.

A few ways in which this can be accomplished include:

Whenever possible, listen first. Adolescents receive dozens of messages from adults during the day. They are given instructions at home, at school, on the bus, during band or ball practice, and many spend their evenings being entertained by the television. When asked, "Who is an adult that you respect and will listen to for advice?" adolescents have a variety of answers from youth pastors to coaches to parents. When asked, "Why this person?" the inevitable reply is that the person really cares. The student will go on to explain that he or she knows the person cares because that person listens.

Students' feelings and thoughts are validated by the person who listens. In times of doubt, fear, or grief, that is the person to whom they will turn.

Communicate that you believe in them. Whenever you talk to an adolescent, no matter what you observe on the outside, you can know that deep within this person is in a difficult period of transition. As a result, they lack confidence in themselves and seek security in their environment.

Students are therefore greatly motivated by the adult who is committed to loving them and who affirms that he believes in them, an adult who sees beyond the outside appearance to the real inner person. Privately and publicly, communicate to your student that you believe in the person he or she is now and is becoming. Help the student discover his or her unique talents and gifts. Affirm your confidence in your student's ability to make a contribution to his or her family, church, and community because of who God has made him or her to be.

3. Practice this principle: there is no quality time without quantity time. Parents cannot simply devote a few *quality* minutes a week to the nurturing of their adolescent. Many parents, including pastors and church staff members, have made the mistake of working so many hours in their career that provides for the family that they have failed to provide what the family needs most: time.

Quality time can be facilitated by:

Being available to participate in their world. Taking the time to drive a group which includes your adolescent to a school or church function, being a sponsor for a special youth night at church, opening your home to your adolescent's friends, attending athletic and social events in which your adolescent participates, and chaperoning special trips are just a few of the ways parents can share in the adolescent's world.

Planning a special evening or activity with your adolescent. Parents who creatively schedule a "ladies night out" or "guys-only camping trips" or "dinner dates" communicate that time with their adolescent is highly valued by them. The ultimate message is, of course, that their adolescent is highly valued by them.

4. Provide boundaries for your adolescent which are consistent with biblical principles, modeling God's holiness and grace if you must discipline him because he has gone beyond those boundaries. Your adolescent needs to learn that, contrary to the culture in which he will become an adult, there is the reality of truth. This truth is God's revealed Word. Boundaries should be based upon commands, examples, and principles found in the Scripture. Ultimately the parent's goal is not only to keep his adolescent from engaging in sinful behavior, but also to nurture a renewed mind whereby adolescents evaluate behavior and attitudes in light of God's holiness and grace.

Whenever you have clearly established a rule or guideline, be firm in disciplining acts of disobedience. Adolescents become insecure when they are able to manipulate their parents, or when they are convinced that mom or dad is just making empty threats. Adolescents want to know what is specifically expected of them and what the consequences will be if they fail. Parents must therefore be willing to be firm.

At the same time, be certain that your firm discipline also

communicates that he or she is not less loved by you. Embrace him or her as your cherished son or daughter even in the midst of discipline.

Engage in dialogue and evaluation with your adolescent about why you have applied biblical principles in this way. Parents should not feel the pressure to always be right. Be willing to listen to your adolescent and work with him to train him in learning to think biblically for himself. Also, be flexible on particulars while always remaining committed to the principles.

5. Promote a healthy adolescent lifestyle in their teenage years. Too many youth are under financial, social, and personal stress to be like "little adults." They need support in being teenagers. This includes time to examine and understand their faith, to consider future careers, and to develop healthy relationships with peers, especially those of the opposite sex.

You can promote this growth by:

Assisting your adolescent in finding Christian peers and supporting his involvement with them. Adolescents want guidance in developing good relationships. They do not want parents to "pick" friends. However, the parents can involve them as early adolescents in solid youth ministries. Junior high adolescents are more open to parents' direct involvement. Begin here with a well-established foundation and slowly transition them into greater levels of independence.

Be prepared to discuss with them not just who to choose as a friend, but also the qualities to look for. Work with them toward a biblical understanding of Christian love and sexuality *before* they are romantically attached to that special guy or girl. To wait until this happens is often too late.

Do not overreact to youth culture. Adolescents want to express their differences. They need to be different than adults. Use wisdom, but do not simply prejudge all as bad because it is different than what you would choose.

A MODEL OF CONSISTENCY

In the midst of the mixed messages of adolescence, parents seek to respond with a consistent message which communicates a love that includes understanding, unconditional acceptance, and wisdom. Parents become an incarnational model of God the Father, from whom such relational qualities are derived. Parents are therefore God's parental love in the flesh. Christian parents who love in this way thus provide adolescents with a context for understanding and experiencing what they most want in life: a love which never fails and never leaves.

EIGHTEEN

Opening Your Teens to God

Kevin Miller

MANY CHRISTIAN PARENTS FEEL THEY—and the faith they want their children to know—get tuned out as soon as their kids hit thirteen. Even the best attempt to share their faith can get turned away.

"It seemed harmless enough." Ted, the father of a young teenage girl, described the scene in his living room the night before.

"Carrie and I were watching a TV show about two teenage girls. The girls were trying to decide how 'far' to go with their boyfriends—what dating behavior was okay. There was absolutely no mention of any moral principles for making the decision.

"So after the show I remarked to Carrie, 'I hope you were able to evaluate that, to decide where you stand.'

"She blew up. She shouted, 'Dad, you just don't understand! This is very realistic; this is how kids feel!' Then she ran from the room.

"I *want* to share my faith with Carrie," he says. "But how?"

FORGET EASY ANSWERS

Forget any just-add-water-and-stir answers. A young teen struggling with the changes of adolescence and a parent facing his own "middlescence" in the same house prove too volatile a mixture. Count on some explosions.

As one mother put it, "There just isn't any recipe for raising teenagers to be Christians. If there were, we would all rush out and buy it." But she and the other parents I've talked to agree on some basic principles underlying how they help their teens open up to God.

THE OUCH PRINCIPLE

"It's *tough* raising teenagers," said one mom. "My wife and I get discouraged at times," admitted the father of two adolescents.

Why the pain? There are at least two good reasons: their adolescence, and your middlescence.

Their adolescence. "The process of growing up involves moving from dependence to independence," explains Dr. G. Keith Olson, in his book *Counseling Teenagers*. "Teenagers must throw off external control enough to allow space for the growth of internal controls."

Your teens are pushing away. It's normal, and necessary— and painful for the parent who remembers the daughter that used to snuggle on his or her lap. But pushing away allows teens to find out what *they* believe, what *they* think is important.

It sounds strange, but this distancing is necessary for them to hold a strong, independent faith later on.

Your middlescence. At the same time children enter adolescence, their parents, usually in their mid-30s to mid-40s, enter a period known as *middlescence.* One experienced youth worker describes it this way:

"Always before, Dad [has been] young, upwardly mobile. There seems to be no end to his potential. Then, in middlescence, he seems to reach that end. His marriage of fifteen or twenty years is dry. Things at work aren't going his way anymore. He doesn't get the promotion he fought for; in fact, he gets lateralled."

Research shows that this period marks the bottom point of all stages of family life: displays of affection hit an all-time low; parental disharmony escalates.

"One of the best ways for you to help your teen is to stabilize yourself. These are two means of stabilizing: First, spend time with other parents of teens, who will understand and empathize. Second, follow the call of those dry yearnings on a journey into deeper Christian spirituality— until you again find "water springing up into everlasting life" (Jn 4:14).

So pain—rather than being a sign that you've failed— shouts that you are the normal parents of a teen. Listen to your pain and seek help; your teen will be helped as well.

THE BORN-FREE PRINCIPLE

A teenager is a little bit like a lion cub. You can raise it for a while, but ultimately it needs to be out on its own. It needs to run free.

This does *not* mean to let your kids do what they want. A recent major study of eight thousand teens and their parents found a strong link between parents who lovingly, firmly discipline and children who have self-esteem, motivation, and religion as a central part of their lives. Teens need parents who care enough to say no.

What the born-free principle does mean is this: teenagers

need the freedom to make some of their own decisions, even if they blow it once in a while. "Every parent wants to shield his kids from potential danger and destruction," says one mom. "But you have to let them stand alone and make their own decisions. They might burn their fingers, but sometimes that's necessary."

"If parents force their kids to read Scripture every day, naturally kids will become rebellious," reminds another mom. "You have to let them make some of the decisions about spiritual matters. You may not always approve of their decision, but you have to let them learn responsibility their own way."

THE OPEN SESAME PRINCIPLE

These guidelines can help you open up a better relationship with your teenager.

Open your mouth. *Campus Life* magazine, a Christian magazine for teens, recently asked its readers: "What one thing happens in your family that you think makes it special?"

You know what teens answered? Good, open relationships. One mom, who practices this principle well, said, "After a big blowup with my daughter, we both need a cooling-down period. But then we talk it out. It may take awhile, but the problem is always discussed."

Open your hands. Dr. Ross Campbell, Christian psychiatrist and author of *How to Really Love Your Teenager*, has this to say: "Provide appropriate and consistent physical contact. Even if a light, brief touch on the shoulder appears to go unnoticed, it registers in their minds."

Open your home. Welcoming your teenager's friends is like welcoming your teen. While they are in your home, open the refrigerator, too.

THE ALL-NATURAL PRINCIPLE

The most persuasive argument for your faith is made day-in, day-out. Teens may forget what you say, but they will certainly not forget what you do.

My father said grace before dinner every day while I was growing up. I don't remember what he said. What I do remember is Sunday afternoons when he would take me to Lucy Butchko's house.

Lucy was wrinkled, shriveled, and in her seventies. Arthritis had twisted and pinned her into a wheelchair. On Sunday afternoons my Dad would visit her, talk with her, and take her to a communion service for shut-ins. That I remember.

One mother described this principle: "I'm almost embarrassed to say it, but my husband and I take the subtle approach to sharing our faith with our teenagers. We try to love them in difficult times. We pray for them. We show them we care."

The natural, daily things you do with your teen will, in the final tally, count for more than words.

THE FOUR-LETTER WORD PRINCIPLE

Pray for your teens. Pray for yourself. Pray for your relationship.

Find healing for your hurts in a God who holds out his hands all day to stubborn, disobedient people. Then pray for your kids.

"You have to pray for your kids," a mother of four teenage boys says, "because you have to let the Holy Spirit work in them. When I get frustrated, I try to remember these words on the bulletin board in my office: 'God doesn't need your contingency plans in case his don't work out.'"

"I go through moods when I'm discouraged about my

daughter," confides one dad. "She doesn't fight going to church, but she would never go to church or a Bible study except by our lead. That's not very reassuring.

"But then I remember that God is at work in families. He deals with families as units, and he intends to save the children of faithful parents. This isn't automatic, of course, but knowing God is committed to our family helps take the pressure off. There's a divine program at work."

CONCLUSION

Maybe the most important thing you can do to help your teens open up to God is simply not give up. "The greatest enemy of most parents is discouragement," counsels Dr. Ross Campbell, "but parents who provide plenty of time, understanding, and love for their teens will gradually see improvements."

At times, your teenager's door may slam shut to spiritual things. But keep knocking; there is One who knocks with you. In time, the door just may open again.

NINETEEN

Guiding Teens to Faith

Jay Kesler

RECENTLY I WAS ASKED, "You've worked with young people all your adult life. What's the biggest problem they face today?" The answer was easy.

At the top of my list is their identity crisis. The normal struggle of "Who am I?" "What am I?" and "Why am I here?" is compounded by information overloading their emotional circuits. The expanding world with its expanding insoluble problems makes them feel even smaller.

Psalm 8:4 asks, "What is man that you are mindful of him?" We can either answer that with—as the next verse says—"a little lower than the angels" or—as the world says—"a little higher than the animals."

Our world teaches young people they are the result of impersonal evolution. But if we accept by faith that we are God's creation and part of an eternal plan, our life takes on a different meaning.

Secular attitudes affect even Christian youth. While they live in a world created by God and are themselves created beings, they have experience-based faith and try to work through dilemmas alone.

I compare the turmoil of today's youth to shell-shocked soldiers who, in the midst of bombardment, start across the field because they can't stand any more fear. Their circuits are overloaded.

Information comes to our youth in mosaic patterns—a splash of truth here, a splash of experience there. Often they can't absorb any more information because they haven't assimilated what they already have. As a result, many live glandular, sensual lives.

CHANGING THEIR WORLDVIEW

We need to help them develop a Christian worldview, based on the premise we live in a *created* world, a visited planet—where God actually walked in the person of Jesus Christ. Knowing him and becoming committed to his teaching and work gives our lives meaning. Suddenly we don't have to solve all the world's problems ourselves—because God is at work. Our task becomes finding his will for our lives and settling into that spot where we can make a contribution.

This idea of making a difference offers emotional freedom for today's youth. Those who can't comprehend that run from their problems.

Most "typical" youth problems—such as drugs and casual sex—are actually symptoms of deeper needs. Lack of purpose causes young people to live for their stomachs and glands, instead of weighing today's decisions against eternity.

How do you reach someone who isn't thinking in such lofty terms, but just wants to gratify desire? We have to meet our young people in a different way than we met them a generation ago. Back then the church met them at the door of unbelief, and debated God and evolution. Today the church is having to meet young people at the door of experience.

But we haven't taken that far enough. After showing

them how to trust Christ as Savior, accept forgiveness, and have the joy of meeting God, we need to put some content to it. Teaching doctrine and the Bible helps them understand that the supernatural has many sides to it. It's not just the great amoebic force they see in the movies.

But most young people don't want to study doctrine. They want to have another party, thereby, sensually experiencing God and Christ. The task of the church, then, is to take them from the door labeled "experience" and bring them to the door labeled "faith." The task is to help them discover a belief system based on Scripture.

THE ROLE OF ADULTS

Parents and youth workers can't just leave kids to themselves; they have to set goals for the young person's spiritual growth. They can't be satisfied that the kids are coming to the youth meetings. The adults must ask themselves, "What are we trying to achieve in this group?"

Of course, kids need fun, but it can be wrapped around the truth, the way chocolate covers a peanut. I tell youth workers, "Do the fun things, but be aware that you're teaching—either directly as you share the Word, or through your life."

The pattern is in the Bible. As Jesus walked with a group of men, he taught them. That's what parenting and youth work is all about. We don't just walk, we walk *and* talk, integrating life and its meaning.

Today that doesn't always happen with teens because middle-class youngsters usually live in a large home, each with his own room. He may have his own TV, stereo, and portable headset. He can *control* the input of his life by turning the dial off and on. Thus, he can become a self-contained unit, totally unsocialized, just living with this electronic input, and becoming its product. This isn't God's intent. He wants humans to interact and learn from one another.

The product of this media age is young people who are illiterate—not only about biblical and historical events, but about life itself—simply because they control the data and select only what they want. We need to find ways of breaking through that, including getting Christian tapes in their collection. The gospel hasn't changed, but our methods of getting it to kids must.

Many parents today grew up during the permissive 1960s. This has affected their parenting. In the general culture, we have a group of parents whose attitudes toward drugs, sexuality, and patriotism are vastly different than those of their own parents, even though they carry the same responsibilities.

Many parents assume the schools will rear their children. But a teacher can rarely help a kid whose parent is irresponsible, a thief, or a drug addict. Parental support has to be present, too. Three things work together: the school, the home, and the church. And many kids have at least two of those unhooked.

That's one reason I shifted from youth work to the family. We have to appeal to the parents to escape their own adolescence.

Christian parents, however, *can* make a difference. It is possible for a parent to say, "Hey, I must have input into my child's life." We won't all agree on what that means—some parents choose home schooling, for example—but each parent has to direct what happens within the family. Even though our society is getting used to things we have no business getting used to, numerous Christian parents are finally saying, "Hey, that's *enough*! We're going to do something about that as a family."

It's the only way we're going to escape what the Scriptures call a "wicked and perverse generation."

A recent Gallup poll said fifty-one percent of churched youth are—or have been—sexually active. So the majority of Christian youth are no different from those "of the world." The statistics are frightening. The Christian kid's attitude toward sexuality *is* largely the same as the general population. Part of this is because current youth work hasn't made a connection between behavior and theology. For many, faith is a way to go to heaven. We've soft-pedaled the idea of responsibility and the behavioral implications of the Christian life. Therefore, our youth look at sexuality like any other life process. Their attitude becomes "If you itch, scratch it." And they don't feel guilty about it.

Christian principles haven't come to them from their churches or their families because they're concentrating on what they can experience. *Knowing Jesus makes me happy. Knowing Jesus makes me free. Knowing Jesus fulfills my longing.* It's like a bromide. The idea of God having a will for our lives and being concerned about how our lives and our behavior affect others hasn't been addressed.

Even at a Christian college, a major task is teaching young people the implications of sexuality, that it's not just about the physical body.

The condom isn't the answer to AIDS. The answer is Christian morality. Abstinence. Monogamy. But our society has given up teaching morality.

Approaching youth as if we assume they're sexually active is tragic. The church needs to teach the value of abstinence and the virtue of virginity. Coming to marriage sexually inexperienced is not an act of *naivete* or stupidity, but purity. We've failed our young people if we haven't told them that.

Some leaders are calling now for a last-ditch effort. It's like the Alamo: Santa Ana's out there with all of his troops marching closer, and we keep moving the sandbags in further and further until it's just Jim Bowie in some room with a knife. It's time we moved those spiritual sandbags back out to the perimeter and made our stand on biblical teaching.

Many parents feel pressured to be lenient. A parent who fears being laughed at by someone saying, "Oh, you're too protective. You've got to let them out and give them a chance," has to realize that what today's teenager is being given a chance to do is become more deeply involved.

This is true not only of alcohol and pornography but also of casual sex. When a young woman has had an abortion—or two—by age twenty, I contend her psyche is scarred. In the past, some parents gave their teens birth control information, ignoring the implications. But AIDS has changed that view. This isn't sowing wild oats; you've sown strychnine.

We need to teach our sons and daughters to be biblically-oriented sexually. I think adults who don't believe that either don't have children and are talking about life in theory, or they've given in to these issues themselves and don't want to acknowledge their mistakes.

Remember the definition of a neo-conservative? Someone whose daughter just turned thirteen. It's true! We become conservative when we have something to conserve. The wrens that have a nest in our yard don't wait until the neighborhood cat is there to decide to give their little ones the acid test. They start by letting the babes take little loops around the nest. When they're able to fly well, they fly away.

This is what we're to do as parents. We teach our children to take these ever-enlarging loops until they can leave the nest. But many children are missing out on those trial runs because of absent parents—whether through divorce, alcoholism, abuse, neglect, or selfishness.

Children need experiences in responsibility. Staying overnight with grandma or with trusted families is a good start. Later, handling money—even doing the math in the parent's checkbook for a couple of months—and caring for pets helps, too.

If the first time a young person has been responsible for maintaining his room or money is when he leaves home, he may not handle it well. That's when people say, "Well, the Army ruined him," or "She was never the same after college."

But the truth is, no independence had been built into them. Young people need to be increasingly trusted with responsibilities—such as the family car. But you don't do that in one big gulp overnight. You start it when they're small. Occasionally those little loops will include mistakes, such as spending money foolishly. But if they aren't given that opportunity, they have to learn the lesson in adulthood when their families will suffer.

THE TOUGH QUESTION

Where's the line between teaching values and blind sheltering? This is a question every parent must *really* think about and then come to a personal conclusion. We can't abdicate our responsibility in this two-pronged situation.

First, each young person either absorbs the two or three feet around him or makes the two or three feet more like himself. If he's an absorber, he needs a safe atmosphere until he develops his own autonomy. Parents need to ask themselves, "Is my child ready to make these decisions?"

Second, today's youth are facing more serious challenges than previous generations. Today's drugs aren't cornsilks smoked behind the barn. And drugs and pornography aren't things they outgrow. It isn't a situation where everybody does a little bit, realizes it was foolish, and goes on. Some of these things can't be moved on from.

Taking the attitude that a young person can experiment

because it's part of growing up is like saying, "We have to teach him about cars by letting him play in traffic."

But in the end, my word to parents is, *be optimistic.* God wouldn't ask us to do something we can't do. All too often we buy into the hand-wringing of "ain't-it-awful?" I'm not into that. I believe that "greater is he that is in us than he that is in the world" (1 Jn 4:4). And if we will put our Christian faith to work—not just as a way to go to heaven, but as a way of life—then it becomes powerful. Christian families—and the church—don't have to give in to the world.

TWENTY

Helping Teens Handle Their Anger

D. Ross Campbell

THE SAD TRUTH IS ALL AROUND US. Many young people raised in Christian homes in America today are not adopting their parents' spiritual values. According to a recent survey of eight thousand Protestant young people, by the time they reach eighteen years of age, only twenty percent of them say they are committed to Christ or will define themselves as Christian. The survey indicated that the remaining eighty percent will have lost their faith in the church and in Jesus Christ. If this decline continues, the future of the church in America is gloomy.

WHY TEENS FALL AWAY

Why are so few young people continuing in the faith? There are several contributing factors. Some children are not taught spiritual values and truths consistently at home. Children learn best at a young age, *before* their teen years when they start to test their parents' values. As they grow older, children are confronted with a society that advocates anti-Christian attitudes. These evil forces take advantage of the normal anti-authority stage of young teens by supplying them with resources which encourage passive-aggressive behavior against parents, church, school, and other symbols of authority.

Parents can combat these anti-Christian influences. They can teach their children at a very early age about the Bible, Christian values, and spiritual truths. As their children become teenagers, parents can acquaint their teens with various evil influences with which they will be confronted and help them understand how to handle these confronta-ions.

To be perfectly frank, the answer to what parents can do to keep their kids from leaving the faith is so complex and critical, I devoted an entire book to this topic entitled *Some Kids Follow, Some Kids Don't.* For this chapter, at the risk of oversimplification, I feel the primary answer lies in the parents' behavior.

Many of us parents fail to communicate our true feelings toward our children in a manner that they can understand. We fail to let them know that we love them—uncondi-tionally, as Jesus Christ loves us.

EMPTY EMOTIONAL TANKS

Kids react more to *how* we behave toward them than to what we say to them. They need positive eye contact, positive physical contact, focused attention, and loving discipline. (I discuss these traits in my book, *How to Really Love Your Child.*) Spirituality is not something which should be kept separate and apart from all other aspects of your child's life. The way in which you help your child handle anger, frustration, and his natural anti-authority behavior during the teen years will affect him spiritually in exactly the same way that it affects him emotionally and psychologically. If you can keep as much anger as possible out of your child's life, his chances of becoming a committed Christian as an adult are greatly enhanced. Ephesians 6:4 states, "Fathers, do not provoke your children to anger, but bring them up in the discipline and instruction of the Lord." The way to keep this anger to a minimum is to understand your child and convey to him unconditional love.

Far too many kids today are running around with empty emotional tanks, and far too many kids today are angry. Pick up any newspaper or watch any television news hour, and you will see that anti-authority attitudes are running rampant in our society. These attitudes, present in your child, will affect his spiritual life. Again, if he is anti-parent, anti-academics, anti-anything, he will also be anti-spiritual. He must have his emotional needs met by unconditional love so that he will not develop damaging anger and anti-authority attitudes.

You cannot force your child to accept spiritual values if he does not feel your love and concern. Many Christian leaders today are telling parents to administer harsh disciplinary actions (i.e., use corporal punishment often) and break the stubborn will of children who misbehave. Such authoritarian teachings result in children who are full of anger, and who rebel against the faith in which they were nurtured.

What's the answer? We must, first of all, love our children and make sure *they know* we love them. Furthermore, we must teach them to handle their natural anger, letting their anger out instead of keeping it inside. Teach them it's okay to say, "I'm angry!" Suppressed anger is a dangerous and destructive element in a child's life.

RECOGNIZING PASSIVE-AGGRESSIVE BEHAVIOR

Passive-aggressive behavior is suppressed anger which a child or an adult displays in a negative, albeit unconscious way. Such anger is *normal* only in one time of life, that is during early adolescence—ages thirteen through fifteen. Passive-aggressive behavior comes from an anti-authority attitude. The purpose of passive-aggressive behavior is to upset the authority figure—to make the authority figure angry. Some examples of passive-aggressive behavior are forgetfulness, dawdling, lying, stealing, chronic lateness, poor grades, and sexual promiscuity.

Younger teens are naturally passive-aggressive to some extent. But if we can handle this phase of their lives correctly, they should mature beyond this stage by the time they are seventeen or eighteen. Thirteen, fourteen, or fifteen-year-old adolescents are unconsciously and some-times consciously, "anti" almost anything. In fact, they are angry about something most of the time. What we must do is keep that anger coming out of their mouths instead of allowing them to keep it inside. This is a very difficult thing for parents to do, because their natural inclination is to quiet their teenagers, suppress the kids' anger, and keep peace in the house. But sometimes I have to ask the parents I counsel, "Would you rather have a son yelling at you or a son overdosed on drugs? Would you rather have a daughter harping and screaming or have a pregnant daughter?" I always tell parents to remove pressure from their teenagers by allowing these kids to verbalize their anger.

Let me clarify one point that might possibly be confusing. I am speaking of *verbal* expressions of anger, not behavioral expressions of anger. I am not encouraging permissiveness in behavior; rather, I am encouraging verbal expressions of anger which can develop into positive methods of resolving anger.

Suppressing anger is something like depressing an in-flated balloon with a bulge in it; if you push the bulge in, it is going to come out somewhere else. Consequently, if we try to keep our children from expressing their anger, it will only pop out in some other area of their lives—in negative, usually passive-aggressive behavior. In passive-aggressive behavior, a teenager gets rid of anger by making his parents upset. So whatever upsets the parents most is what the kid is going to do. What would upset Christian parents most? Where is the primary interest in most Christian homes? It is in spirituality, of course.

THE "ANGER LADDER"

In order to deal with the complexities of resolving anger, I have created an "Anger Ladder," which is explained more fully in my book, *How to Really Love Your Teenager*. There are fifteen rungs on the ladder, each one representing a better way of expressing anger. Climbing up the ladder, we come to verbal release of anger, aimed at anyone within hearing distance. As poor as this behavior may sound, it is an improvement over passive-aggressive behavior. The top rung of the ladder is the most positive method of resolving anger. This method involves direct, but respectful, rational expression toward the person against whom the anger is being directed. Parents should try to help their teens progress toward appropriate expression without pushing them back down into passive-aggressive behavior.

Expect your teen to become angry at times, and encourage him to express it verbally. Then, determine where he is on the Anger Ladder, and work with him from there. Find a time after you have both calmed down to praise your teen in the areas in which he expressed his anger correctly, then ask him to correct the aspects you think need changing.

HANDLING ANGER APPROPRIATELY

All of us have felt anger and have felt the need to release anger by yelling or talking to someone. Imagine how you would feel if you were told not to yell if you hit your thumb with a hammer. What if your spouse refused to listen to your tale of a bad day at work, or ignored you when you wanted to comment or voice your opinion on a subject which upset or angered you? Wouldn't that be frustrating and make you angrier? That is how our children feel when we don't really listen to them, especially when they are upset or angry.

Therefore, as parents we must listen to our children and let them express anger verbally. We can help our teenagers to "nip it in the bud" if their anger is based on misunderstanding. Alternatively, if the anger is justified, we must help them verbally vent it in a slow, positive way so that it can be resolved. This method of anger resolution does not come naturally to anyone. We, as parents, must patiently train our teens to manage their anger in a mature way. We must guide them toward positive verbalization of their anger, rather than allowing behavioral outbursts.

It takes time and patience, but who is more important than your child? No talent at all is involved in telling your child to shut up. Our natural reaction may be to strike a child when he opens his mouth in disagreement. Unfortunately for parents and children alike, too many child-rearing experts are advocating that very practice. This teaching is often detrimental, because it prevents a child from getting through the normal passive-aggressive stage. He remains passive-aggressive into adulthood. An angry adult cannot be a productive person. He cannot accept authority of any kind, including spiritual authority. "For man's anger does not bring about the righteous life that God desires," (Jas 1:20).

We, with God's help, can reverse the trend of kids lost spiritually by raising and relating to our children and teenagers in the proper manner. We can help keep their hearts open and receptive to a personal relationship with Christ, so that God can mold their character and their lives.

TWENTY-ONE

Responding to Youth Culture

Richard R. Dunn

"JOEL, WHERE DID YOU GET THIS MUSIC?"

"Mom, what were you doing in my room? You don't have to be checking up on me all the time, you know. I'm sixteen years old now. I think I deserve a little privacy."

"Joel, I just went to your closet to get your dirty clothes and I found this CD cover lying on the floor. I was *not* 'checking up' on you. Besides, the question is not, 'What was I doing in your room?' but 'What are you doing with this type of music?'"

"Mom, there is nothing wrong with that CD. It's a new metal band. They are really great."

"How can you call a band named *Thrash N' Slash* 'great'? I've heard that a lot of those bands are Satanic, and this group sure looks like it fits that description."

"SATANIC! Give me strength, mother! A lot of the guys at church have this same CD. Surely you don't think Jerry, Clark, and Barry are satanists."

"I'm not saying anybody is a satanist. I'm just saying that I don't understand why you would be listening to a group like this. It doesn't seem like a very positive thing for a

Christian young man to be doing."

"Mom, there are *Christian* metal groups, too. So, what's the big deal about how they look? I enjoy their music like a lot of my friends, and it doesn't hurt me to be listening to them. It's not causing me to start doing drugs or stop going to church. It's just music!"

Rock music, music videos, movies, fashion fads, and a strong emphasis on peer social relationships are key elements of what has been termed "youth culture." Contemporary expressions of youth culture offer a plethora of potential conflicts for the Christian parents of an adolescent. Like Joel's mother, parents may confront adolescent behavior and attitudes which they perceive as incompatible with the Christian lifestyle they want their teenager to be living.

Parents who are committed to working through such confrontations with their adolescent son or daughter must consider a number of issues. The first concern is, "Why is this important to my teenager?" To answer this question, parents must begin with an understanding of the roots of youth culture and why adolesents are so strongly affected by what their peers consider to be "rad" or "in." The second area to be addressed by the parent is, "What are the most effective and appropriate responses to my teenager's involvement in these elements of youth culture?" Parents need to be equipped with principles to follow as they seek to nurture their adolescent as a Christian disciple in a secular culture. It is important to consider in advance how to confront these issues so that parental responses become a preventative measure for keeping minor parent/teen conflicts from escalating into full-scale wars.

Joel's mother has many things on her heart as she reflects on this confrontation with her son. She knows she could win the battle by demanding that Joel trash *Thrash N' Slash*. Joel's mother also knows that the way she responds as a Christian parent has implications not only for Joel's relationship with her but also his relationship with God, his Heavenly Father. As the old saying goes, she may "win the battle but lose the war." What she most wants is for her and Joel both to be winners by preventing the war from ever occurring.

ROOTS OF YOUTH CULTURE

Adolescence can be described as a time of transition. Teenagers are no longer children, but neither are they adults. They are experiencing the dynamic changes which result from a maturing body, an expanding mind, and emerging, surging emotions. The end result will be as dramatic as the metamorphasis of a caterpillar.

The process, however, does not take place in the safety of a cocoon. On the contrary, this transformation occurs primarily in the context of social relationships with peers who are experiencing similar personal upheaval. These peer relationships are expressed in familiar forms such as boyfriend/girlfriend, cliques, and peer social norms. Youth caught in the swirling changes of physical, mental, and emotional maturity seek security and personal identification within this social context.

Consider the nature of the transformation Joel has been experiencing. Since he turned thirteen just three short years ago, he has witnessed incredible changes in his internal and external world. Joel's body has gone through rapid development which has been both dramatic and traumatic. He has grown eight inches taller, gained fifty pounds, and added four shoe sizes during this time. He has also completed his primary sexual development during this short span so that Joel's body is more of a man's body than that of a boy.

Joel's mental maturity has been just as dramatic, though the changes are not so immediately observable. Joel can now evaluate life from an abstract point of view. As a boy, he believed what his parents believed and identified with their values. As an adolescent he finds himself asking, "Why?" about everything which is important in life. In addition, this new mental capacity allows Joel to think in terms of another person's perspective. In other words, Joel can play through his mind what his friends at school may be thinking about him as they see him in the cafeteria or in the hallway. His peers become the mirror by which Joel most often views himself.

Joel and his peers are described as being *egocentric* because they are so concerned about how the world and others relate to them. No longer children, not quite adults, they are pursuing a personal identity which will enable them to say, "This is who I am." Their self-image comes from their perceptions of how others are viewing this new body and person. It has been said that adolescents view themselves in these terms: "I am not who I think I am, I am not who you think I am, I am who I think you think I am."

Peers, therefore, take on the role of most immediate influence, as adolescents are striving for independence and personal identity development. Peers provide what Joel would consider to be his life support system. He needs to be differentiating himself from his parents, becoming his own person. Yet he is not ready to be a fully self-sufficient adult, although this sounds better than being fully dependent like a child again. Thus, Joel first looks to his friends for feedback on how he looks, acts, and presents himself. For Joel, the biggest fear in his life is that his friends would reject him.

Youth culture consists of the specific expressions and norms of this peer influence. Youth culture thus results from the adolescent identification process. It functions as a source of guidelines and expectations for someone who does not want to be seen as a child, but who lacks the maturity to be an adult. Rock music, social norms, and fashion fads become symbols of nonadulthood and nonchildhood. They provide an opportunity for teenagers to be distinctively adolescent. Thus, a statement against what is considered to be *their* music or *their* friends or *their* styles may feel like an attack on their sense of security, independence, and personhood. It's no wonder that when they feel threatened in these areas they often dig a trench and prepare for war!

INGREDIENTS AFFECTING YOUTH CULTURE

Before considering principles and methods for responding to the various elements of youth culture, parents therefore start with a consideration of the importance of peer influence. An empathetic look into their world allows us to reflect upon how it must feel for them to even think about the possibility of being labeled as "nerd," "geek," or "loser" among their peers. But there are other important considerations which should also be placed into the mix from which a recipe for appropriate responses can emerge.

First, negative peer influence is not the only force at work within the adolescent world. Many have called for a "positive peer pressure" within the church youth ministries which will offset the opposing forces of secular expressions of youth culture. This is what should be thought of as an "almost" great concept. Peer pressure implies a bending of behavior against the will or at least against one's best judgment. The term "positive peer influence" is a more accurate picture of the teachings of Jesus about what it meant to be a disciple. Christian parents should not just be concerned that their teenagers do not "smoke, drink, chew, or run with those who do." Rather, these parents' ultimate desire is that their son or daughter have a mind that is not conformed to the world but has been transformed (Rom 12:1, 2).

Second, it is often difficult to discern an adolescent's motives for his actions. For instance, one student attends a questionable movie with all of his friends from school. He neglects to ask for parental input because it doesn't seem to be a big issue. His best friend, however, has a strong sense that his parents would disapprove and has decided that he can probably go without them finding out. The former is simply not thinking about the implications of his actions, the latter is very aware that he is being rebellious. Yet, both would probably respond to confrontation with the same answer, "I didn't think you would mind." Thus it takes time and energy to differentiate between what was a careless act expressing independence and what was a willful choice to be rebellious.

Third, some seemingly "innocent" actions may produce very harmful results in the long run because of the prevalance of sin in contemporary culture. This generation has been described as being "at risk." They live in a dangerous world full of traps which are appealing to the lusts of all men and women (1 Jn 2:15-16), especially to those who have yet to form their sense of self and are searching for ways to fit in and feel good about themselves through positive peer feedback.

Finally, adults too quickly blame adolescents for creating the unhealthy elements of youth culture. Adults, including parents, often fail to realize that it is adults who are pushing the movies, music, clothes, materialism, and sensuality onto the students for the purpose of making a financial profit from them. This does not excuse adolescents from responsible choices. Yet it is a call to all Christian adults and parents to take the responsibility to help our youth stand counterculturally as disciples of Jesus Christ. It has taken a lot of adults to create the chaos we are in, and it will take just as many, if not more, to begin working it out.

RESPONDING TO YOUTH CULTURE

The key to effective and appropriate parenting during conflicts over questionable elements of youth culture is to focus on the issue rather than reacting to the symptom. As the following principles and life applications illustrate, there are ways to develop a partnership with your maturing adolescent that allows the young person to change not only behaviors but also to be transformed by the renewing of his mind in Christ.

1. Don't react with private investigation, respond with personal understanding. Adolescents are quick to be defensive when they perceive that any adult is entering their world because they are inadequate to make good decisions. If they feel that you are simply trying to find out information in order to prove your theory that they cannot be trusted, they will place an invisible, personal "wall" to keep you out. You become a threat to their sense of self.

Rather than conveying the image of the private investigator who wants an immediate description of what they are doing and why they are doing it, use the "personal understanding" approach. If you have questions about what you have observed in their attitude or lifestyle, begin with an attempt to understand how they are feeling about this and what experiences are influencing them toward this questionable element.

- Sarah Hamilton's parents were concerned with the way she had been dressing lately. Her Mom felt that the outfits she was borrowing from friends were all tacky and some of them even made her look like she was a "loose" girl.

  Mrs. Hamilton's first reaction was to ask Sarah why she was wearing such unattractive, inappropriate *borrowed* clothing when they had provided her with such nice clothes. A few days later at breakfast, Mr. Hamilton looked at Sarah and remarked that "no daughter of mine is leaving this house dressed like that." An argument ensued that ended with Sarah tearfully running upstairs to change clothes though not without a maximum protest.

  That evening Mrs. Hamilton asked Sarah if she could talk with her about the issue of her clothes. Mrs. Hamilton wanted to interrogate Sarah in order to find out who had convinced her to make this drastic wardrobe change and put a stop to this terrible influence. Instead, however, Mrs. Hamilton asked her if they could talk together about what type of style Sarah was interested in wearing now. She told Sarah that she would like to find some common ground concerning what was acceptable so that Sarah could consider herself fashionable, but not violate certain standards which she and her father felt were essential.

2. Don't react with communication killers, respond with interpersonal dialogue. There are a number of "communication killers" which prevent parents from bridging the gap of understanding which often exists between them and their adolescents. These "killers" are deadly to the process of personal understanding and only solidify personal walls which may be present in the relationship.

First on the list is the *cliché.* Parents deplore adolescent clichés such as, "Everybody else is doing it" or "It's my life." In the same manner, adolescents balk at such destroyers of dialogue as, "Because I said so" or "If you had to work for a living like your father" or "If I've told you once, I've told you a thousand times!" (Now a thousand and one to be precise!) These statements are used because they create a "no win" situation for the other person. Interpersonal dialogue requires responding with comments which encourage—not discourage—the other person's expression of personal thoughts and feelings.

Second on the list are *comparisons.* A sure way to defeat an adolescent's attempts at expressing what he is experiencing is to use the old reliable, "Your brother doesn't act this way" or a variation on the old reliable, "I bet Suzanne doesn't say things like that to her father."

Third on the list is a combination of the first two. It usually begins with the dreaded, "When I was your age..." Even in small doses, this statement has the same effect on an adolescent as a general anesthetic.

Many others could be listed. The point is, deliberately work toward *discussing with* rather than *talking at* your adolescent. Carefully guarding against these interpersonal communication assassins will help you get past the surface and into the heart of the matter.

- Betty Markham is a single mother who has a fourteen-year-old son, James, and a ten-year-old daughter, Samantha. Betty relies on James to help by watching Samantha before and after school. Lately, James has been getting less and less reliable. She has been frustrated with him for being irresponsible and is concerned about the friends he is hanging around with at school.

  Tonight she came home to find him at a neighbor's house. He had Sarah with him, although he knew they were not to leave the house. Even worse, he came home wearing a T-Shirt filled with gargoyle-like creatures bearing the logo, "HOUNDS OF HADES." She was angry, shocked, and even a bit frightened at the boy whose appearance and behavior seemed to have changed in a matter of days.

  Betty wanted to sit James down right then and give him a four-hour lecture. "How could he do this to me?" she thought to herself. "After all I've done for him and he is turning out just like his father." She only got angrier as she reflected on what her non-Christian neighbors must be thinking of this boy from the only Christian home on the block. Then Betty remembered her father who had been a Christian but also a man with a temper. She remembered four-hour lectures (they seemed that long), and how they turned her away from him for years, a turning-away which included abandoning her Christian values and getting into a marriage which ended in grief.

Betty knew James would have to be punished, but she also knew that what was on her son's heart and mind was more important than what was on his shirt.

3. Don't react with the Bible as power tool, respond with biblical truth relevant for decision-making. Scripture is God's revealed truth and is invaluable in teaching us about who God is, who we are, and how we should live as his children (Ps 119; 1 Tm 3:16-17; Heb 4:12). It is authoritative and perfect. Therefore, it is our best resource for developing principle for making decisions which please our Lord.

The Bible can also be misused. For instance, its commands and examples can be presented in such a way that they frustrate the listener with impossible and irrelevant applications. Adolescents need to understand the Bible as it relates to their context. To simply say, "The Bible says that you should not act that way, Billy" only alienates the adolescent. Unless Billy is able to find the link between the wisdom and truth the Bible offers in the reality of his daily life, he will feel like the Bible is an adult tool for pulling rank on him.

- Jerry was very concerned about the way his son, Matt, was behaving with his teammates on the soccer team. Jerry knew that most of the guys were not Christians. Matt had spoken earlier in the season about the pressure they put on the sophomore guys to be attending parties with them where there was a lot of drinking. Matt had assured them that, as a junior, he was immune to their teasing and mocking.

  Jerry had noticed Matt becoming much more comfortable with those guys and even joining them for post-game pizza at a local restaurant. Last night Matt came home later than usual from such an evening. This time he smelled like cigarette smoke, and Jerry thought he even smelled a trace of alcohol. He informed Matt of his concern, and indicated they would discuss it in the morning.

Jerry was sitting at the table when Matt walked in the kitchen for some juice. He asked Matt to sit down, and they began to discuss what had happened the night before. Matt said he had gone to a party for a while, but that he had not had anything to drink. He only went because his friends invited him and he was tired of always saying, "No."

After listening for quite a while, Jerry said, "What do . . ." He had intended to ask the question, "What do you think Jesus would do in that situation?" At that moment, Jerry realized that even he did not know exactly what Jesus would have said, and besides, their suburb was nothing like Galilee. He realized the statement might make an important principle sound like a Christian cliche.

Instead, he began again. "Matt, I know you are facing a tough time with this situation. I want to support you by helping you make the right decision. I've found some Scripture which has been useful to me when there seems to be no clear direction to take. How about you and I getting together this weekend to read those verses and discuss how they may apply in this situation? In the meantime, if you have some verses you want to add to the discussion, write down the references. It may take us some time to come up with an answer as to what you should say or do next time you are invited to a party, but I think this situation is worth taking that time."

4. Don't wait to see how you will react, prepare your response. Nothing great was ever achieved on the battlefield or ball field, in the courtroom or classroom, without preparation. The same is true for parenting an adolescent, especially in regard to the area of youth culture.

Preparation for success in responding to adolescent involvement in areas of tension includes: (a) establishing clear guidelines about what is considered to be an absolute standard; (b) being consistent in your responses to violations of well-defined rules and guidelines; (c) making yourself available to discuss possible changes in expectations as the adolescent matures; and (d) outlining in advance a strategy for resolving potential conflicts which may arise in the future.

- Ben and Nancy Goodman have two sons, Benji, who is 13, and Barry, who will be 11 in two months. Recently Benji has been talking more about movies which his friends have been watching as well as movies he would like to see. The Goodmans are a bit concerned because their standards in relation to movies seem to be different than the standards of many of Benji's friends' parents, including some of his friends at church. They realize that as the boys grow older this will become more of an issue.

  Ben and Nancy have called the boys together for a family discussion about what should be the "Goodman Movie Policy" for the teenage years. They have indicated that they want the boys to be able to spend time with friends and see some of the movies their friends watch. They have also communicated their commitment to help Benji and Barry learn to make good decisions about movie viewing. After presenting the policy, they plan to listen to the boys describe their thoughts and feelings regarding its guidelines.

  The Goodman policy differs according to age. From twelve to sixteen, movies which get a "G" or "PG" rating at the box office are acceptable unless there is some specific subject matter, such as demonic themes, which are apparent in the content. From twelve to sixteen, all "PG-13" movies will have to be reviewed by the parents through reading a Christian periodical resource which reveals the content of the movie. A decision will then be made based on this review with both teenager and parent having input, and with parents having the final say. From sixteen to eighteen, "PG-13" movies will become acceptable, again subject to parental review. During these years, "R" movies will have to be reviewed by the parents, with the understanding that permission to view an "R" movie would be the rare exception. These guidelines are to include the rental of videos as well as attendance at movie theaters.

Breaking of these guidelines will be considered a serious violation. However, the boys are encouraged to review all movies and decide for themselves, through discussion with their parents, whether even the movies which are allowed are really a valuable use of their time and money as well as being compatible with their Christian lifestyle.

RESPONDING REQUIRES A RELATIONAL PERSPECTIVE

Paul's writings always seem to be great at getting to the "bottom line." When he wrote to help Timothy deal with the attempts of certain Ephesians to wed the myths of their culture with the truth of Christ, Paul explained how to recognize God's truth, "The goal of this command is love, which comes from a pure heart and a good conscience and a sincere faith" (1 Tm 1:5).

Parental responses to youth culture require the same "bottom line." Ultimately, Christian parents are fulfilling their stewardship as disciplers of their children as they progress through the difficult transition we label "adolescence." Parents are therefore committed to biblical truth being known and experienced by their teenagers. Yet the application of this truth into individual lives is a process. It will not happen because you always say or do the right thing. It will develop through your willingness to listen, to love, to offer flexibility without compromising truth, and to prayerfully respond. Prayerful responses must be focused on what is happening in the heart, conscience, and faith of your son or daughter rather than merely reacting to behavior that you do not understand or find offensive. Thus parents become the unsung heroes of the adolescents' lives, not by winning battles over them but by loving them enough to fight the battles with them.

TWENTY-TWO

When a Child Strays

Marshall Shelley

NO MATTER HOW SOLID THEIR RELATIONSHIP with their children, most parents still feel a tremor of anxiety as a son or daughter leaves the nest. What kinds of choices will he or she make? What if these choices are foolish or self-destructive? What if the young people need help to avoid a terrible mistake but don't want it or don't have the strength to accept it? The years after high school can be a time of awkward transition—a twilight world between accountability and independence.

What follows is the story of one family that agonized over that tension. Not all families would choose to handle this situation the same way. But this family's story holds some vital clues for others in similar situations.

Bill and Maryann Harris had worked hard over the years to raise their three children in the Christian faith. Living as Christians came relatively easy for the two oldest children.

After going to college on a football scholarship, Martin went to seminary and became a church-planter, and Brenda attended a Christian college and joined the staff of an inner-city youth ministry. While both were confident, capable workers, neither was quite as strong-willed as the youngest, Caryl.

Through her high school years, Bill and Maryann considered Caryl's self-confidence to be one of her greatest virtues. Her standards were high. She didn't want to limit herself to dating one guy. "I don't want to be seen as anyone's 'property,'" she would say. She enjoyed going out with a guy from church one night and a guy from school the next night—"double dating," she called it.

Maryann and Caryl often talked about the guys Caryl was seeing. "Some of the girls at school have to sneak out to see their boyfriends," Caryl said. "I wouldn't want to date anyone I wasn't proud to bring home to meet my folks."

After high school, since Caryl enjoyed making her own clothes, she decided to attend a school that offered courses in fashion design. She enrolled at a state university two hours from home. It was far enough to afford some independence, but close enough to allow visits home once a month. In addition, during her first year, Caryl would call home every week with another story about dorm life. She especially enjoyed telling about her attempts to be a Christian in a secular setting.

One night she reported the following conversation with two of the guys on her floor, Mitch and Tony, who had come to her room.

"Is it true what we hear—that you don't drink alcohol?" they asked.

"It is," said Caryl.

"You mean you've never had a beer or a glass of wine?"

"I don't even drink Nyquil!" Caryl laughed.

"I can't believe it!" Tony said.

"I've never met anyone who hasn't had a drink," said Mitch. "We'll have to change that!"

"Why?" Caryl countered. "You have all kinds of friends who drink. Wouldn't you like to have one friend who doesn't? After all, wouldn't it be nice to have someone who can drive straight after a party?"

Before they went back to their own room, the guys had admitted she had a point.

Bill and Maryann enjoyed the story. They encouraged Caryl to keep trying to fit in without violating her standards.

"A campus is a tough place to be 'in the world but not of the world,'" Bill told Maryann after putting the phone down. "But it sounds like Caryl's doing a pretty good job."

Caryl met with some Christians in her dorm once a week for breakfast, Bible study, and prayer. She also attended a Tuesday night Bible study for college students at the Baptist church near the campus.

Bill and Maryann suspected nothing unusual, then, when Caryl called one week during her sophomore year to say that "a couple of guys in the dorm are in love with me."

"They've already sent me a dozen roses and a box of chocolates," she said with her characteristic laugh. "I marched down the hall and gave them back the chocolates. I told them my figure couldn't handle the calories, but I did appreciate the flowers."

"Which guys were they?" Maryann asked.

"Mitch and Tony."

"Isn't that an unusual gift for them to give you?"

"Oh, I don't know," said Caryl. "We've got a pretty close group here on the floor. It's sort of nice; it's been a while since any guys have shown a special interest in me. Maybe I've been spending too much time in the library." She laughed. "Don't worry, Mom. They're harmless."

Over the next few weeks, Bill and Maryann kept hearing more and more about Tony and Mitch, especially Mitch. Caryl reported on conversations they had at supper. She mentioned that Mitch offered to walk her home from Tuesday night Bible study.

"Mitch is in the Bible study, too?" Maryann asked.

"No, I invited him, but he says he's not the 'religious' type," Caryl replied. "He just doesn't think I should be walking across campus alone at night. Besides, he's usually coming back from the library, so it's not out of his way. I appreciate the company."

Whenever Caryl went to football games or out for pizza, Bill and Maryann noticed, Mitch's name was usually mentioned as part of the group.

During Christmas break while Caryl was home, the university's basketball team was playing a local college. Mitch was in town to see the game and invited Caryl to go with him. "I'm not all that keen on going with Mitch," she told her Mom, "but since I've met some of the basketball players at school, I do enjoy seeing them play."

When Mitch came to pick her up, Bill and Maryann met him for the first time. Bill's first impression was that Mitch's west Texas accent made him sound almost a hayseed. His boots and Stetson added to the image. Mitch was a preveterinary student, and he seemed friendly enough, asking, "Should I get Caryl back any time in particular?"

"I appreciate you asking," said Bill. "Just keep it reasonable."

After Mitch and Caryl had left for the game, Bill told Maryann, "He seems like a nice guy, but hardly Caryl's type. They're from totally different backgrounds. She says he gets good grades, but you'd never know it by listening to him."

That night after Mitch brought her home, Caryl told Maryann, "We had a good time. Mitch really knows basketball, and he explained the strategy real well. And afterward, since Mitch knows all the players, we went out to eat with them. I felt like an 'insider.' I do wish he hadn't ordered his beer; I don't usually go out with guys who drink, but he's a sharp guy and maybe I can be a good influence on him. He could use a Christian friend. He said one of the reasons he likes me is because I have strong moral standards."

In the weeks that followed, the Harrises heard more and more about Mitch—about the new Ford pickup he drove, about his dreams of establishing his own veterinary hospital, about the times he took Caryl to cattle and horse shows. "I only wish he'd clean up his language," said Caryl.

Bill and Maryann didn't say much about the budding friendship until one day Caryl mentioned that Mitch teased her a lot about going to the Bible study. He called Christians "the Great Pretenders," suggesting they live in a make-believe world. Caryl said, "I told him that wasn't true, that *I* was a Christian who tried to keep her feet on the ground." Mitch's response was "Well, you're okay, but all the guys at that Bible study are flyweights."

"I didn't have an answer for that," Caryl said. "I had to admit none of the guys in the fellowship are real sharp."

"It's too bad he can't meet some of the Christian athletes who've spoken at our church," Maryann said.

"Yeah," said Caryl, somewhat absently.

"He's not out to undermine your faith, is he?" Maryann asked.

"Oh, Mom, don't be paranoid," Caryl said. But for the first time, Maryann felt a flutter in her stomach.

When Caryl told her parents that Mitch continued to try to get her to go drinking with him, Bill and Maryann suggested that maybe Mitch wasn't the friend he seemed to be. "If he knows your standards, why does he keep trying to get you to change them?" Caryl didn't have an answer.

Apparently, she mentioned to Mitch that her parents were not overjoyed with their friendship. The next time she called she managed to work into the conversation that "Mitch was asking me if I felt restricted growing up in a preacher's home, if my parents always chose my friends for me. He told me his parents gave him a free rein." Bill and Maryann chose not to debate the issue, feeling that they didn't need to defend their approach to parenting.

In February, Bill got an invitation to preach at the Baptist church next to the university, and Caryl brought several of her dorm friends, including Mitch, to hear him. Mitch seemed relaxed during the service, but afterward Caryl said,

"Mitch was pretty uncomfortable. He had never attended anything but an occasional church service before, and he didn't even tell his folks he was coming with me today." All of them were encouraged that at least he came. But the experience seemed only to prompt increased antagonism from Mitch.

"I don't see why you go to that church," he told Caryl. "They're so narrow. They take their religion too seriously."

"It *is* important to us," said Caryl. "But that doesn't mean we're fanatics. We enjoy life, too. We just want to enjoy *all* of life, including spiritual life now and eternal life in heaven."

"But it's different from the way I was raised," he said. "We're religious, too, but we party and have a good time. And my parents don't continue to try to control my life."

When they heard about that, Bill and Maryann began to fear that Mitch was not only attacking Caryl's faith, but also trying to sabotage her relationship with them. "But maybe we *are* being paranoid," Maryann said. "She does have to grow up." Bill remained silent.

What they both did notice, however, was that when Caryl called home, she wouldn't mention Mitch unless she was asked, and even then, Bill and Maryann got the impression she didn't want to talk about him—a definite change from a month before.

During spring break, Caryl came home for the week, and Mitch stopped by one night to take her out. When they returned around three A.M., Mitch's loud good-bye—spinning tires and a blast on the horn of his pickup—woke Maryann. She slipped on her robe and went downstairs.

"Sorry about the noise, Mom," Caryl said, laughing nervously. "Mitch is a little rowdy at times."

"How was your evening?"

"We had a good time."

"I'm glad. Where did you go?" Maryann asked, trying not to appear the inquisitor.

"We saw a movie, and then went out to, uh, a place to eat."

"A place I should go sometime?"

"If you must know, Mom, it was The Fiddlestring. It's a country music place that Mitch really likes. He likes to two-step. It's fun."

"I thought you had to be twenty-one to go there."

"You're supposed to be, but they didn't check our I.D.'s."

Maryann decided to wait until morning to say anything more.

At breakfast, Bill and Maryann pointed out that Caryl had changed considerably from the time when she took pride in being the only one in the dorm who didn't drink, to now, when she was defending Mitch for taking her to a bar, even though she was under age.

"I didn't drink. I just went to dance," she said.

"Seems to me it's living a lie just being there," said Bill. "And I don't like you riding with Mitch after he's been drinking. You used to look down on the kids in high school who snuck off to drink and spend time with boyfriends. You've changed."

"I guess that's just the way I am," Caryl said. She refused to admit any wrongdoing or say she wouldn't do it again. Bill and Maryann hoped this was just one of those minor crises of growing up and testing her independence. They wanted to tell Caryl to stop seeing Mitch, but they weren't ready to risk their increasingly strained relationship.

For the rest of the school year, though slightly defensive about Mitch, Caryl was still open about their activities. She mentioned that late one night he knocked on her door, and she could tell he was drunk so she refused to let him in. "He sometimes gets violent and throws things when he's been drinking," she said.

She mentioned that he'd asked her to wash his truck, so she did. She was watching her weight because Mitch had said something about her pants getting tight. And she told how the Bible study group was demanding more time, and she thought she was going to have to drop it from her schedule next year.

Bill and Maryann hoped that the summer break, when Mitch returned to his Dad's veterinary clinic and Caryl came home to work, would also mean a breakup in their relationship. But it didn't. They may have been apart, but the weekly letters and phone calls showed the ties were still there.

"Maybe we should accept Mitch as a given and try to work with him," said Maryann.

"Go ahead," said Bill. "But their relationship will never work. They're too different. I just wish Caryl could see that."

That fall, they told Caryl to invite Tony and Mitch home for a Sunday afternoon picnic. When she did, however, Mitch told her, "I don't have to go there. I've already met your folks." Bill wondered what had caused the hostility. After all, they had only met face-to-face twice by this time. Whatever the reason, throughout Caryl's junior year, the hostility between Mitch and the Harrises increased, trapping Caryl in the middle.

At the beginning of the year, Caryl had said, "I'm going to be twenty in October. Let's plan something fun for my birthday." So Maryann began making plans: a party on Saturday night with some high school friends and a Sunday dinner with some friends from their church.

On Tuesday, however, Caryl called to say, "Mitch wants to take me to Dry Lake this weekend to celebrate my birthday."

"But we've planned a celebration here," Maryann said. "Can't you cancel?"

Maryann took a deep breath and said, "No, we can't."

"Well, Mitch isn't going to like this. He wants me to go home and meet his parents."

"I'm sorry," said Maryann, not used to being this forceful. "Everyone's already invited. I think you should come home."

Caryl finally agreed, but as she predicted, Mitch was furious. "You can't make any decisions yourself!" he shouted. "Your parents make them for you. They rule your life. They'll never set you free. You're a slave." Caryl denied it.

Mitch stalked off, swearing. "Forget you, woman. You're hopeless."

When she came home that weekend, Caryl said, "I've done a lot of crying the last couple of days. It's over between Mitch and me; I had no business going with him anyway. I actually feel relieved." Maryann felt relieved, too, but Bill suspected the war was not yet over.

For her birthday, Bill and Maryann let Caryl take their second car, an aging Ford Fairmont, back to school. She had a part-time job in a fabric store, and now she wouldn't have to walk or ride buses at night—or get rides from Mitch.

Mitch ignored Caryl for two weeks and then suddenly reentered the picture, ready to pick up where they'd left off. He asked her to type one of his papers. Caryl said okay. Then she helped him wash his truck. Soon they were dating again, and she was cleaning his room and doing his laundry. She bought cowboy boots and jeans "because Mitch thinks they look good on me" and began wearing red fingernail polish "because Mitch likes it."

"And he accuses us of keeping her a slave," Bill muttered to Maryann after one of the weekly phone calls.

Caryl did put her foot down at times, although feebly. After one party featuring "chugging contests," Caryl told him she didn't feel comfortable around drinking games and would not go to any more of those parties.

"You better learn to like them," he said.

"I don't think I have to," she replied, but as the months went by, she stopped resisting and went wherever he wanted.

At every opportunity, Bill and Maryann were encouraging her to break off the relationship, to spend more time with friends from the Bible study.

"Caryl, we just don't see any future in this," Maryann said. "Mitch is really very, very different, and I don't see any hope that he's going to change. We've prayed for him. And remember when you told him why you were a Christian? You shared your testimony, and he said, 'Don't you ever talk to me like that again. I like the way I live. I'm not going to change.' Until he shows some sign of softening, there's really no solid foundation for a relationship to be built."

Without being absolutely demanding, they tried everything they could: pointing out areas of incompatibility and insensitivity, trying to clarify Mitch's tendency to be critical of the faith, raising questions about the direction things were going.

"Mitch seemed to have more and more power over her, and she wasn't able to break it," reflected Maryann. "She would say, 'Well, there are no Christian guys who are interested in me' or 'There are no Christian guys who have the same charisma he has. He's so masculine; he takes charge.' She complained about Christian guys, but since she'd stopped going to the Bible study and church activities, she wasn't any place where she could meet them. Her life revolved around her small circle of friends in the dorm."

One night, over the phone, Caryl said, "I like Mitch because he has goals. He knows where he's going."

"Assertiveness may be attractive to a certain point," said Bill. "But I think you'll find it can become oppression and control four years into marriage. With him you would be a non-person."

"All the Christian guys I know are losers," she said. "Non-Christian guys treat me better than the Christian guys I know."

"As a male, it's hard for me to respond," said Bill. "But I do know it's not worth mortgaging your soul for any relationship with a man."

As Bill recalls, at this point things seemed to become less rational. "Caryl's emotional responses didn't seem to have any pattern. One day she seemed to agree that she wanted to live the way she'd been brought up, but then the next day she would be angry at us for raising any question of right or wrong."

Mitch graduated the Christmas of Caryl's junior year and went to Argentina to work with an uncle on a cattle ranch. The Harrises breathed a sigh of relief, thinking perhaps he was gone. He did write Caryl several letters, a few of which she let Maryann read.

"He used so many obscene words I was embarrassed," Maryann told Caryl. "Doesn't he care who he's using that language around?"

"Oh, that's just Mitch," Caryl said.

"How can you stand it?"

Caryl just shrugged.

When Mitch returned to Texas, Caryl was home for spring break. One evening around five P.M., he phoned to see if she was free for dinner. She said yes, but Mitch didn't show up until after ten. Caryl met him at the door. Maryann stood in the background.

"Here I am. Let's go eat!" he said to Caryl, without a glance at Maryann.

"You haven't eaten supper yet?" asked Caryl.

"No. I'm famished. Let's go." And he grabbed Caryl's hand and pulled her out the door. Maryann walked to the door and watched the pickup spray gravel as it sped away.

When two A.M. came and went, Bill said to Maryann, "I didn't use to worry about Caryl when she stayed out late, because she would always tell us what happened when she got back. But I don't trust Mitch. And after Caryl's been with him, she doesn't like to talk about it."

It was after three by the time they got back, and Bill was lying in bed unable to sleep. Maryann, also restless, had stayed up to invite Mitch to spend the night on the downstairs couch. Caryl's hair was mussed and her clothes disheveled.

"Late supper," Maryann said in her most matter-of-fact voice.

"Oh, you know," said Caryl. "It took a while to eat and talk and stuff."

"Well, Mitch, it's too late to try to make it all the way to Dry Lake," Maryann said, trying to retain her composure. "I've fixed the couch for you to camp out." Mitch accepted with a simple, "Sounds good."

The next morning, Caryl was up early, hair curled and make-up on, and went to McDonald's for breakfast with Mitch. When they came back, Maryann was in the kitchen, but Bill stayed in his study, trying to read. "I don't think I should see Mitch," he had told his wife. "I don't know if I'll be able to control what I would say."

Caryl walked in to where her mother was reading the newspaper.

"Mitch wants me to go to Dry Lake with him," she said.

Maryann gulped. "I don't think it's a good time to ask after last night, but ask your father." Caryl went upstairs.

Bill said, "Absolutely not. Mitch has earned neither our trust nor our respect. I can't give you my permission." Caryl protested but eventually went downstairs to tell Mitch she couldn't go.

"Well I've never been treated like this before!" Mitch fumed. "Your Dad won't even talk to me himself. I guess that's what happens in religious circles."

When he left, neither Caryl nor her parents felt like saying anything to each other. But Maryann tried. "It would take a lot, I know, but if Mitch could become a Christian, it would be like the apostle Paul. He'd sure have a lot of energy and drive to give."

"It'll take just as great a miracle, and until it does," Bill said, looking at Caryl, "it can be dangerous for a Christian to be too close to him."

Maryann turned to Bill. "But don't we have to keep befriending him? If we tell him to leave Caryl alone, what will he think of Christians? What if he winds up in hell because we didn't want him around?"

"Your opinion of God is too small," Bill sighed. "If God is sovereign, I doubt if he's going to allow two parents' concern for their daughter's spiritual life to send someone else to hell. God has plenty of ways to reach Mitch—including Caryl's life standing for something else."

For the rest of the school year, Caryl stayed at the university, and the Harrises could only pray she was making wise choices. Mitch was in Dry Lake, but they knew he made periodic visits to see Caryl. Caryl had mentioned that Mitch had a serious side—he was even talking about how many children he'd like to have. Bill and Maryann didn't know what to say.

That summer, Caryl found a job near the university and decided to stay in Austin. She came home on weekends once or twice a month. One day while Bill was at his office, he looked up to see Mitch standing in the doorway.

"I thought it was time we talked face-to-face," said Mitch.

"That sounds like a good idea," Bill replied.

"I want to know why you don't like me," Mitch demanded.

"We don't dislike you, Mitch. But we can't encourage a relationship between you and Caryl when there is no solid foundation for a lasting relationship. We see such fundamental differences in the way you two were raised."

"Like what?"

Bill tried to explain the differences between Mitch's nominal Christian upbringing and Caryl's active evangelical family. He tried to explain conversion, forgiveness, and living a life that honors God. "Being a Christian is a way of life for our family," he concluded.

"Caryl's told me all that," Mitch said. "I come from a strong family, too. We believe in God and go to church once in a while. There's not that much difference in our beliefs."

Not wanting to deny Mitch's religious heritage, Bill said,

"I think I mean something different by commitment to God than you do—it's more than church attendance. I just wish I could explain it more clearly. But Mitch, even if it were true that our religious differences were minor, which they aren't, I think the difference in our backgrounds is such that you two could not be permanently happy together. Part of it is the difference between rural and urban expectations. Part of it is Caryl. You have a strongly traditional view of a woman's role in the home. Caryl has been raised to think for herself, but she has not been herself since she's met you. She's taken by your strong personality, but that won't last in a marriage. Eventually she would feel oppressed. The bottom line is that you two don't belong together."

Mitch reiterated his opinion that they were two grown adults, and he was sure they could work out any differences. He rose to leave. "But I do understand a little more of your opinion," said Mitch.

"I hope I've made myself clear," said Bill. "I appreciate your stopping by."

Both Mitch and Bill left thinking they had won a major battle. Bill told Maryann, "I think Mitch may see we've got good reasons to be opposed to their relationship." And Mitch told Caryl, "I think I got your Dad straightened out on things."

The next weekend, when Caryl was home, she said to her mother, "I'm glad things went so well between Mitch and Dad. Mitch said Dad is starting to come around."

"That isn't how I read it," said Maryann. "Dad and I are as opposed as ever. We've prayed that this thing would work out, that Mitch would change. But the only person we've seen change, Caryl, is you. You used to be proud of your standards. Now you're defending Mitch—the places he takes you, the language he uses, and the attitude he has toward us and everything we stand for. It can't go on like this."

Caryl patted her mother on the shoulder. "Don't make such a big deal out of it, Mom. I'm a big girl now. I can take care of myself." She changed the subject to her job, the money she was making, and the minor repairs the Ford needed.

That night Maryann told Bill, "I'm afraid Mitch is winning the war. We may be losing our daughter. When Martin and Brenda left home and got married, it was sad, but we rejoiced with them, too. But if Caryl leaves like this, it would be only tragedy." Even after praying together that God would protect Caryl both from herself and from Mitch, neither of them slept well.

The rest of the summer, Caryl was increasingly preoccupied. "She looks like she's in a dream world," said Maryann. Bill noticed that her comments about people in the church were all negative—"They're a bunch of losers"; "I'm glad I'm not going to church every Sunday anymore"; and "The people in the bars are friendlier than the people in your church." That shook Bill.

When the young couples' Sunday school class invited him to speak at their annual "family life" retreat, he declined, even though he had enjoyed doing so in the past. "It would be pure hypocrisy for me to talk on family life, especially on parenting, when we are failing with one of our own children." Even his enthusiasm for preaching was gone.

By the middle of August, when Caryl started talking about trying to find a job in Dry Lake after graduation, Bill and Maryann decided something had to be done—even something drastic.

"We may be writing off our daughter," said Bill. "But unless something is done, we've lost her anyway. We've got to do something, even if Caryl leaves us, to restore the emotional stability of this home."

He sat down to think of all the leverage points he had with

his daughter, who was now less than a year away from college graduation and complete independence. He put his thoughts into a letter:

Dear Caryl,

Sometimes being a parent is close to pure joy—like watching you take your first steps, taking part in your baptism, celebrating your selection as yearbook editor, or seeing you living out your faith as a college freshman.

Other times being a parent means having to make some difficult decisions, and now is one of those times.

Caryl, your mother and I feel like we're losing you. You think you are old enough to make your own decisions, but we'd like to think the way you were raised would have some influence on those choices. Over the past two years, we've talked repeatedly about your relationship with Mitch. Your family backgrounds, religious backgrounds, and personalities are incompatible. We cannot accept him in our family. And you would soon be torn between living in two worlds.

We've asked you to break it off. You have refused. You have said, "I'm old enough to make my own decisions." Maybe so. But if you continue in this relationship, Caryl, we will assume this means you are ready to make those decisions—and accept their consequences. You will always be our daughter, but once you remove yourself from under our guidance, there will be certain changes in our relationship.

1. You will no longer have use of the family car. We will expect you to return the Fairmont immediately.

2. I will tell the company we no longer need the $1,000 scholarship they provide for you each year.

3. My own financial support of your education will end.

4. During your upcoming internship this year, you will not live in our house, as previously assumed, but you will find and furnish your own apartment.

5. Upon graduation, you will not be living with us "until a job opens up" but will immediately be on your own.

As you learned to say in your self-assertiveness courses, Caryl, "I'm a self-made woman." Perhaps you are. I just thought you should know all that's involved if you persist in being your own person.

Let us know by August 30 if you prefer life with Mitch or life as part of our family.

Sincerely,
Dad

The Harrises mailed the letter, and three days later, August 27, Caryl called. "Well, I got your letter yesterday," she said.

"Have you done anything about it yet?" Bill asked.

"I thought I had some time."

"You have three days. We have to settle this, Caryl."

"I know, Dad." Caryl was subdued as she hung up.

Maryann noticed the strain on her husband's face. "She still wants to play both sides," she said.

"Yes, and I'm removing the option of the second side," he said.

I less than ten minutes, the phone rang again. It was Caryl. She was crying.

"I just called Mitch and told him it's over. I told him I'd gotten a letter from my Dad and that I knew I had to decide between him and my family. And I realized I love my family more. So I did it. . . ." She broke off in sobs.

"Do you want us to come be with you tonight?" Maryann asked.

"Yes."

Immediately Bill and Maryann packed a few things and drove the two hours to be with Caryl. When they arrived, Caryl hugged them both, but weakly. *She looks wrung out,* thought Bill. *But then, I feel like a wet noodle, too.* Over dinner, Caryl asked, "If I've done the right thing, why does it feel so bad?"

Bill and Maryann tried to affirm her decision. "You must

feel torn apart," Maryann said. "You've chosen one side of who you are—the way you've been raised. It's painful when another side of you is cut out."

"We don't mean to be cruel or to punish you," said Bill. "We're simply trying to clarify what has really been taking place. Caryl, I'd rather hurt you now than to see you torn apart in a miserable marriage five years down the road."

After that emotionally draining crisis, the Harrises hoped everything was over, but their resolve continued to be tested. One Sunday afternoon when Caryl was home and Bill was away speaking at another church, Mitch called, inviting Caryl to meet him at a friend's apartment across town.

"Can't I go?" she asked her Mom.

Maryann's throat felt dry. She wondered how Caryl could ask after all they'd been through. "I thought we agreed everything was over."

"But I need to talk to him. If I can't go there, can he come here?"

"I wish you wouldn't, but you do what you think is right."

Caryl told Mitch to come on over. Within fifteen minutes Mitch was saying, "We're going out to a movie."

"I can't allow that," said Maryann.

"Don't you think Caryl's damn well old enough to make up her own mind?"

"When it comes to certain things, no," said Maryann, surprised at her own bluntness. "We've made it clear we don't think this relationship will work, and we don't see any point in you taking her out. If you need to talk, you can do it right here."

Mitch and Caryl went into the family room and sat on the couch. Maryann walked by and noticed Mitch's arm around Caryl. They looked quite cozy. Taking a deep breath, she walked in and said, "Mitch, I don't know if you realize the importance of what Christ has done in our lives and what it means to us to be Christians, but I'd like to explain it if you're interested."

"Go ahead."

Maryann had just finished her church's evangelism training course and went through the whole presentation of the gospel. When she finished, Mitch said, "That's what I believe too. But, dammit, I get tired of having it crammed down my throat!"

"I'm sorry if it sounds like preaching," said Maryann. "But we try to live according to the Bible, and it commands us not to be 'unequally yoked' to those who don't share our commitment to Christ."

"My family worships God," said Mitch. "I don't see why you worship an old book written back in the 1300s."

Maryann chose to overlook this historical error.

"We feel there's another way to live when Christ becomes the Lord of your life. You live either to please him or to please yourself. That's why we think you and Caryl would have serious problems down the road."

"Hell, Caryl's no different from me."

"That remains to be seen. At least the way she's been raised is different from your lifestyle. You've made fun of her friends; you've made fun of her church and her parents; you've tried to undermine our relationship with her. It seems to me you're pulling her down instead of building her up. You once said you were attracted to Caryl because of her strong morals, because she was different from other girls you dated. It looks to me like you're trying to change her from the very thing that attracted you in the first place."

He looked a little surprised but said, "My parents weren't for this relationship at first, either. But they met Caryl and learned to like her. I don't see why you can't do the same."

"Mitch, you've taken her places she wouldn't have gone otherwise. She never dated anybody who drank or who used the language you use. Just sitting here tonight, five times you have used language we find vulgar or blasphemous," and

Maryann repeated the words. Mitch's mouth dropped open. "You seem to be content with that. That's your lifestyle, but it isn't ours, and I don't think Caryl would be content with it either."

"You have no right to judge me. You're the most closed-minded people I've ever met."

"I don't mean to judge. I just wanted you to hear our side."

The conversation turned to other, less volatile topics, and Mitch showed no sign of leaving. Maryann didn't budge either. *If they stay until three in the morning, I'm staying here too,* she thought. But finally after midnight, she said, "Well, I think it's about time you left, Mitch, because Caryl has to get up early to head back to school, and she really needs her rest."

I can't believe I'm doing this, she thought, *I've never asked anybody to leave my home before. But if he's exerting emotional energy, I will too.*

Mitch was civil as he got up and said good-bye. Afterwards Caryl, who had been silent throughout the evening, said, "I was terrified, Mom. Whenever I tried to talk with him like that, he'd tell me to shut up. I hope he listened."

"Me too, dear," said Maryann. "Me, too."

But even that was not the final encounter. Bill's resolve was also tried when two weeks later, he drove home from the church one afternoon to find a pickup truck in the driveway and Mitch talking with Caryl on the front steps.

"I had only the distance from the intersection to the house to find some emotional equilibrium," Bill said later. "I was fearful. I was angry. I was disappointed because we couldn't seem to get this thing behind us. Mitch insisted on coming by, and Caryl didn't have the strength to say no. So I had to play the bad guy."

Bill pulled into the driveway. As he walked to the front door, he tried to keep his voice from shaking. "Mitch, what are you doing here?"

"Just a social visit," said Mitch.

"I'm going to have to ask you to leave."

"Why? Let's go in and talk about it."

"There's nothing left to talk about, Mitch. I resent your appearing here when we've given you a full explanation before."

"What about Caryl? Doesn't she have a say?"

"I'll talk to her when you're gone," said Bill.

"Shouldn't I be a part of it?"

"No, Mitch. That's just it; you're not a part of it." Bill paused, because as a pastor the next words were some of the most difficult he'd ever had to say. "You are no longer welcome in this house. I don't want to see you here again."

"Well I stayed away for three weeks."

"Mitch, you don't cut off a dog's tail a little bit at a time. It's time you left."

"Damn you!" Mitch shouted, his face fiery red. Unused to facing a will as strong as his, he stormed out to his pickup, and his departure left rubber on the driveway.

Inside the house, Bill found Maryann crying, Caryl pale, and his own voice quivered when he asked, "Caryl, why was he here?"

"He phoned to ask if he could come over, and I said yes."

Bill shook his head. "Why do you think I wrote that letter a month ago? Caryl, maybe it's time you moved out. I'd though we'd reached the bottom line, but apparently we haven't."

Caryl's eyes filled with tears.

"I don't know what you want with your life or which way you want to go. But we are at the end of our emotional tether. We can't go any further. And if it means you're not going to be a part of our family any more, we're prepared to face that, even though we don't want to. But we cannot have this emotional warfare continuing. We're that serious. I don't want to see him in this house again."

"I can't make any decision right," Caryl sobbed. "Anything I do is wrong. You're disappointed in me. Why should I go on living? I'm good for nothing."

"Caryl, Caryl," Maryann said softly, holding her daughter's hand. "That's not true. It's because we think so much of you that we've done this."

"You've got too much to offer to throw it away on a guy like Mitch," said Bill. "The only reason you've lost your confidence in yourself is because for three years Mitch has been tearing you down. He's made your decisions for you. He's a mood-altering drug, and when he gets out of your system, you'll be able to make good decisions again."

For the next year, Bill and Maryann had to repeatedly prop up Caryl's sagging self-worth. But they persevered, and Mitch at last stopped his attempts to see Caryl. Gradually Caryl returned to the confident, independent thinker she had been.

Now, four years later, she has thanked her parents several times for stopping her from making a big mistake. She's the manager of a fabric store and helping direct the high school ministry in her local church.

"We took drastic action," Bill said. "It wouldn't have been successful if there weren't a hundred messages—a thousand messages—before that we loved her and truly wanted the best for her. We risked our twenty-year investment in family building. We clipped our emotional coupons with Caryl, and this is something you can do only once. It's not a threat you can use over and over. I'm not sure it would be the right approach for everyone, but in our case, it was the right move."

WHEN YOU RISK THE RELATIONSHIP

Bill and Maryann Harris faced a unique situation with a daughter who did not want help with a particular relationship. Not everyone will encounter the same factors. Not everyone will choose to handle even similar situations the same way the Harrises did. But the story of the Harris family does illustrate several transferable principles, some of which have been suggested earlier in this book, for helping those who don't want help. What are the things Bill and Maryann clearly did right?

1. They showed support and love. For almost twenty years, Bill and Maryann had built a strong relationship—with one another and with Caryl. Even when the tension came, they continued to support Caryl (though not her decisions) and maintained their relationship with her through months and years of nerve-wrenching conflict. They demonstrated their care for her even when they were knocking heads.

2. They communicated clearly and specifically. They told Caryl their reasons for disapproving of her relationship with Mitch, and they made clear their expectations for her to break it off. They did not simply hint at their feelings or speak in veiled, off-hand comments. Clear communication is critical so that when the bomb is dropped, the person doesn't feel it's a complete surprise and knows how to move to keep from getting hit.

3. They did not rush to judgment. Bill and Maryann were slow to escalate the conflict, to raise the stakes. They reserved playing their trump—risking their relationship—until they had exhausted every quieter, more diplomatic means available. They refused to rely on drastic measures (or threats of them) until they were absolutely sure Caryl was on a destructive path and all other methods of helping her had failed. They went the second mile, and the third, and the fourth ... before acting. Only when the risk of losing her through confrontation was less than the risk of doing nothing and letting her be hurt even more, did they put their relationship on the line.

4. They showed the extreme measures were for her best interests. As Bill put it, "I'd rather hurt you now than see you torn apart in a bad marriage five years from now." Bill and Maryann had carefully checked themselves to make sure their actions were motivated not out of self-protection but genuine concern for their daughter's welfare. Then they were free to tell her so with boldness and integrity.

5. They gave her a choice. Even when they wrote the admittedly drastic letter, Bill and Maryann respected Caryl's freedom and let her make the final decision. They could have written, "Because of your previous actions, we are now cutting you off financially...." But they didn't. They spelled out the consequences of her actions and gave her the freedom to make her own decision accordingly.

6. They set a time limit. They gave clear boundaries to their position—the behavior desired, the course they would follow if it were not chosen, and the time limit for the decision. They didn't let the Sword of Damocles hang over Caryl's head forever.

7. They backed the demands with resolve. Bill and Maryann were prepared to take the necessary measures, as wrenching as they would be, if Caryl's choice went against them. Empty threats are worse than doing nothing at all. Both Bill and Maryann demonstrated their strength of will and their determination to follow through on their decision.

8. They did not withdraw once the decision was made. The Harrises did not begrudge Caryl the pain she had caused them. Once she had made her choice, they dropped everything and drove to see her. They supported her, helped her stand firm in her choice, and continued to intervene with Mitch. Choices are not made in an emotional vacuum. They require maintenance. Bill and Maryann offered themselves to help Caryl maintain her decision.

Helping people who don't want help usually does not get to the point where the relationship must be risked, fortunately, but when the situation arises, these principles point the way to the greatest chance of success.

Part 6

Teaching
Christian Behavior

TWENTY-THREE

Instilling Moral Values

Jean Lush
with Pam Vredevelt

A RE VALUES CHANGING? Some say yes, and the changes in many ways are not positive. One retired schoolteacher said, "Twenty years ago if a student was caught cheating, it was embarrassing to the student. The student didn't want his peers to know. Last year when I caught a boy cheating, his reply was, 'You didn't tell me I couldn't cheat!'"

William J. Bennett, former secretary of education, has said that Americans want schools to do two things: teach our children to speak, think, write, and count; and help them develop standards of right and wrong to guide them through life.[1]

While some claim that it is important to form character at school, others claim it can't be done. Bennett says, "Some educators deliberately avoid questions of right and wrong or remain neutral about them. Many have turned to 'values' education theories that seek to guide children in developing their own values by discussion, dialogue, and simulation—a tragically mistaken approach, since research indicates that it has had no discernible effect on children's behavior. At best, this misguided method threatens to lead our children morally adrift."[2]

If Americans agree there is a profound need for moral development among children, how can this be accomplished? First, we must look to the home for some answers. One of the most important tasks of parenting is guiding children through moral development. Dr. Thomas Likona says, "Most parents want their children to be intelligent, talented, and attractive. These nice things add to the lives of children, yet if they do not possess all of these qualities, they can still 'stand tall' as human beings. If, however, they are not good, decent people, can they 'stand tall'?"[3] My answer to this question is, "Probably not."

I have talked with scores of mothers who have asked me, "How can I raise my son to be a man's man and at the same time help him develop tenderness and compassion toward others?" or "How can I nurture a competitive drive in my boy and at the same time guard him from becoming too power-hungry?"

THE STAGES OF MORAL DEVELOPMENT

For over a dozen years, psychologist Lawrence Kohlberg followed the development of moral knowledge among seventy-five boys in the United States and observed moral knowledge in other cultures as a comparison with his sample. Based on his findings, Kohlberg says moral development occurs in three major states: preconventional morality, conventional morality, and postconventional (or autonomous) morality.

Kohlberg believes preconventional-stage children are guided by pleasure, pain, and the satisfaction of their own needs. They respond primarily to punishment and reward. This first stage occurs from birth to age twelve.[4]

During this phase of development, parents must consistently teach their children what is right and wrong in relation to their wants. For example, most two-year-olds like to explore driveways, sidewalks, and streets. If one ventures out into a parkway, the parent naturally tries to catch the child and say, "Johnny, that's a no-no. If you go out in the street, you might get hit by a car!" The two-year-old concludes a "no-no" is wrong and everything else is okay.

After the age of six, most children think in terms of what they can give and get in a situation. They obey for the sake of winning a reward. It is very important for parents to consistently follow through with promised rewards. If they don't, they send their children mixed signals. Double messages dangerously confuse children. I've seen too many little boys totally throw out their parents' rules because obedience didn't get them what they were promised.

In the next stage, conventional morality, Kohlberg says children judge their actions in terms of being good and respecting authority. The child moves beyond himself to consider his family, peers, and the world at large. His moral choices are based on guilt and peer pressures. This phase takes place between twelve and twenty years of age.[5]

The young adolescent is moving into a period of life when he begins saying to himself, "I should or shouldn't do this or that." He has a sense of right and wrong based on what he has been taught in his family and among his peers. Having shaped his sense of right and wrong in younger years, parents must consistently support his good moral choices in the teen years. An adolescent needs to hear his parents say, "I am proud of you for making a good choice" or "I am disappointed in your poor choice." He also needs to understand *why* his parents think his choice was right or wrong. This helps him internalize standards and paves the way for him to move into the third stage of moral development.

Kohlberg's final stage of moral development, autonomous morality, occurs in adulthood, if at all. In this stage the individual tries to find general principles to govern his actions and the actions of others. He internalizes morals for himself, develops selfless concern for others, and is conscious of his rights and responsibilities in society. In Kohlberg's multicultural study, very few subjects ever reached this stage of moral development.[6]

The big question here is: where will the child get his standards? For Christian parents, the answer is obvious: biblical principles become the guide and building block for moral attitudes and conduct.

BUILDING A GODLY MORAL FOUNDATION

Christian parents have a challenging job. Nearly everywhere their children go, they are exposed to anti-Christian beliefs. We live in a very complex society that does not promote biblical morals. Television, music, and the media pump children full of information that is anything but Christian. The prevailing philosophies of this age are: "Look out for number one. You only live once, so grab all the gusto you can get. If it feels good, do it!"

What can Christian parents do to counteract these values and build a godly moral foundation for their children? The following suggestions can provide a start.

1. Clarify your own values. Before parents can develop morals in their children, they need to define their own values. What is important to you? Whatever you value, your children will value. What do you want for your children?

Most parents desire their children to be fair, honest, and trustworthy. They want them to know about kindness and compassion and their opposites. They want them to respect the rights of others and feel a reasonable measure of concern for their fellow man. They want them to recognize greed and overreaching ambition, as well as know that hard work pays off. These are godly values.

2. Help children demonstrate your values. If you want your son to grow up to be considerate and respectful of women, teach him to act considerately as a child. Have him hold the car door for his mother and sisters. Show him how to assist them with their coats, seat them at a table, and not start shoveling food until the hostess has taken her first bite.

If you want your son to become a man who brings happiness to others, give him opportunities to do this while he is growing up. Beth, a single parent, used to make a big deal about her birthday and Mother's Day. About a month before the celebrations, she began saying things to her children like, "I can't wait for that wonderful birthday cake and all the cards." I was a bit bewildered by her actions, because they were so foreign to her usual unselfish attitude. One afternoon my daughter asked her why she made such a fuss over her birthday. I've never forgotten her reply. She said, "To be honest, I don't care a bit about my own birthday. And you know I have never been a cake-eater. But I want my boys to learn to be considerate and honor others. If I teach them to honor me on occasions like this, maybe they'll think of others when they're adults."

Beth also insisted her boys visit their grandparents and take presents or baked goodies to them on holidays and birthdays. She said, "I can't make them feel tenderness toward others, but I can help them demonstrate acts of caring. If I don't take the lead and show enthusiasm about bringing happiness to others, why should they ever bother?" Sometimes her boys didn't care for the fuss over family birthdays (when it wasn't their own), but Beth didn't back down. She kept telling herself, "Someday, the push will pay off."

And it did. The last time Beth and I talked, she told me one of her sons was engaged. A few weeks before, his fiancee had completed a hard year of school, and he sent her a huge bunch of red roses. That was quite a sacrifice for a young man on a limited budget, and proof that Beth had accomplished one of her goals.

When her boys were young, the senior pastor of her large church requested to see the boys individually. Every six months they "reported in" about their behavior and told how they were honoring their single mother. Beth didn't always know what was said in the meetings, but she said they made a tremendous impression on her boys and reminded them of their accountability to others.

Beth creatively taught her sons to bring happiness to others. Another mother inspired her son to serve with his talents. For several years I have admired a brilliant young medical surgeon who lives near us. He excels in everything he does. His mother says he never gave her any problems while growing up, and his wife adores him. His friends and acquaintances say he is one of the finest people they know.

I talked with Jack, this man, recently, and asked him, "Why are you such a giant of a man? Everyone who knows you boasts of your greatness."

He told me something about his mother that intrigued me. When he was a young man, she taught Jack that he had superior gifts. His IQ was on a genius level; that was apparent to everyone. He was also unusually strong and handsome. Jack said his mother told him, "Since you have many gifts, you have an obligation to be great, honest, and to serve mankind. You have not earned these gifts. They were given to you. What you are on the inside must be as superior as the talents that show on the outside." To this day, those words ring in his ears and motivate him to excel in his work and relationships.

Lorraine, a mother of three children, wanted her children to honor Sunday as a family day. She said, "My husband and I felt Sunday should be a peaceful time for our family to be together. But somehow it always turned into a day full of noise and commotion, the same as any other busy day. Steve and I decided we needed to be more passionate about sticking to our convictions, so we went about making some drastic changes. We told the children that Sunday was to be strictly a family day. No playmates were allowed to come over, and the children were not to leave the house unless the family went together."

Lorraine was amazed at the effect this had on their family. Everyone slowed down, read more books, communicated more, and became better friends with one another. Now she says, "As parents, we need to fight for our values. Once we decide something is important, we must work hard to give those values high priority."

3. Be an example. Morals are better caught than taught. The best way to pass on values to your children is through living them. As one father put it, "You've got to *be* it, not just talk it." If you want your children to show respect for others, treat them with respect. Listen without interrupting. Use "please" and "thank you." Walk alongside them, not ten yards ahead.

Andrew Murray, one of the greatest Christian writers of the past one hundred years, was a father of a large family and preached many sermons about raising children. He quotes the proverb, "Train up a child in the way which he should go . . ." and says, "Training comes far more through example than precept. The atmosphere of a well-regulated home and the influence of self-control exhibited by parents unconsciously set their mark on a child. When parents give way to impulse and temper, perhaps at the time when reproving or restraining the child's temper, the effect of their good advice is more than neutralized."[7]

When parents model moral behavior for their children, they need to keep in mind that attitudes are just as contagious as actions. If I make my children go to church, read the Bible, and pray, but don't demonstrate my own love for church, reading my Bible, and praying, I might be doing more harm than good. They may learn a legalistic list of *dos* and *don'ts* rather than develop a personal love for God.

A parent's words must also agree with his actions. If you want your children to be generous, don't pass up opportunities to put something in the offering plate or give love offerings to the needy. If you want your children to share the Lord with their friends at school, talk about Christ with your neighbors and friends who don't know him. If you want your children to forgive others, you must forgive and ask them for forgiveness when you make mistakes. If you want your children to be free of prejudice, they must see you extend yourself to those of different races and colors. If you want your children to be truthful, don't take home the excess change the grocer gives you. Instead, use the incident as a chance to teach them that honesty is more important than an extra ten-dollar bill.

4. Encourage your children to develop their thinking skills. When moral dilemmas arise, ask them questions like, "What is the problem? What happened to you because of your behavior? What happened to others? What other choices did you have?"

You can also help them learn how to think by reading stories with a moral message. When characters are forced to make a moral choice, stop the story and ask your children what they would do if they were in the same situation. Find out why they would make that choice, and then help them look at their decision in light of God's Word.

5. Educate your children by telling them what you believe and why. Most of us make statements like, "My mom used to say . . ." or "My father always emphasized . . ." A young doctor I admire told me he spent many days with his grandparents while he was growing up. He thought they were magnificent people with very high standards. In everything he did, he wanted to please them. When I asked him if he had urges to cheat in school, as many boys do, he said, "I could never have cheated, because I knew it was totally against my grandparents' beliefs, and it would hurt them too much." Children need to hear their elders talk about their beliefs.

6. Pray for your children. One of the greatest tools parents can use for shaping their children's lives is intercessory prayer. If we want our children to cling to godly values, we must pray not only for their physical and emotional development, but also for their spiritual progress. In today's society, it isn't enough for parents to simply be good examples. They must go a step further and call on God to guide and protect their children, to buffer the ungodly influences that press in on them, to accomplish his purposes in their lives, and to enable them by his Spirit to live according to the guidelines they have learned at home. God says, "Call to me, and I will answer you, and I will tell you great and mighty things, which you do not know" (Jer 33:3 NAS). "The prayer of a righteous man is powerful and effective" (Jas 5:16 NIV).

Assisting children in their moral development is not an easy task. It requires parents to live close to the Lord and to lean on him for divine understanding and guidance. Andrew Murray once said to a group of parents, "No grace of the Christian life is obtained without sacrifice; parenting, or the influencing and forming other souls for God, needs special self-sacrifice. Like every difficult work, it needs purpose, attention, and perseverance. . . . Our duty as parents is never measured by what we feel is within our power to do, but by what God's grace makes possible for us. And we cannot know fully what grace can enable us to do, until we begin."[8] The good news is, when we're helping our children develop godly morals, we can rest assured that God is always eager to assist us with his supernatural resources.

ENDNOTES

1. William J. Bennett, *Human Events* (January 31, 1987), 100.
2. Ibid., 101.
3. Ruby Friesen, "What About Morality?" Beaverton Family Counseling Center *Counselgram* (Winter 1988).
4. Harry Munsinger, *Fundamentals of Child Development*, 2d ed. (San Diego: Holt, Rinehart, and Winston, 1971), 448.
5. Ibid., 448.
6. Ibid.
7. Andrew Murray, *The Children for Christ* (Chicago: Moody Press, 1952), 110.
8. Ibid., 67.

TWENTY-FOUR

Instilling Holy Ambition

John W. Yates III

E VEN THOUGH I GREW UP IN ONE OF THOSE HOMES where President Kennedy wasn't too popular, his family's commitment to serving humanity is exemplary. This isn't true only of Jack, Bobby, and Teddy but, to an extraordinary degree, the new generation of Kennedys has demonstrated the same sort of commitment to public service and a sense of ambition to hold public office. Every time you turn around it seems another Kennedy is seeking election. Why? They have demonstrated that it is possible to shape the ambition of the entire family.

Ambition *can* be a negative characteristic. It is sometimes self-seeking and ruthless. But ambition for good is desirable, and ambition to put our gifts to work for Christ is commended by Christ. In the Lord's parable about the talents Jesus commended the ambitious servant and was clearly disgusted with the cautious one who only wanted to play it safe.

I want my children to make a significant impact on the world for the sake of Christ. How can I instill in them this sense of holy ambition? How can I help them develop a passion for a Christ-like life and a vision for their own personal ministry without "playing God" in their lives?

These are questions that have been pushing me to do some serious reflection, and particularly since I spent some time with an unusual man. Let me tell you about him.

He was still in college—half my age—and while he showed appropriate respect for me, he was perfectly at ease with me as well. He wanted to learn all he could about me as well as from me, and he talked of himself and his own life as well but not in a self-congratulatory sort of way. He enjoyed my company and I his, but he was equally at home with my children. He and I traveled together a bit, and I was struck by his courtesy and thoughtfulness as well as by his engaging ways. He wasn't the least put off by some rather difficult characters we encountered—he seemed to be himself and enjoying himself with all sorts and conditions of folks. I found myself wondering "was I this mature and well adjusted at his age?"

He was responsible in the duties assigned and seemed to have mature judgment about what was important and what could wait. An obvious natural leader and superb athlete, I could find no trace of conceit or false humility. His attitude toward his family and parents struck me as sensible and healthy—clearly devoted to them and committed to them, with deep respect for them as well, yet at the same time he could laugh about their eccentricities, teasing them and loving them.

I have not met many young men like this one. Have you?

Perhaps what impressed me as much as any of these things, however, was his spiritual maturity—his love for God was genuine and he was in the process of building his young life and shaping his large dreams about a set of priorities that, from my perspective, were right on the mark. He had a deep biblical faith and a clear sense of who Christ is and who Christ calls us to be. He was seeking to make a mark wherever he was—on the campus, at work on the weekends, coaching the little kids at the soccer camp he had started, or wherever. Aware of his youth, he seemed to me to be committed to becoming all he could be for the sake of Christ. I loved his sense of ambition because it wasn't self-seeking—it was more the holy sort of ambition we see so clearly in St. Paul's life and letters.

Do you know any young people like my young friend? You probably know quite a few with strong and special gifts. Likely you know some others who are unusually mature. But how many youth do you know who have a deep and clear sense of wanting to make a significant impact on their world—their peers, their generation, and their era—for Christ and Christ alone? If you can name more than one you are unusual.

Can we instill holy ambition in our children?

Will our children love Christ and his kingdom deeply? Will they follow and obey him? Will they trust him? Will they dream dreams for Christ's sake or purely for their own profit? Will they seek to influence those around themselves to come to the Savior? Will they look at life from God's perspective? Will they put their many gifts to work to build the kingdom of God? In short, will they long to be all God wants them to be, accomplishing his purposes, pursuing his mandates all their lives? Or will they settle for a sort of mediocre materialistic milksop sort of Christianity?

We cannot know. But as I have observed unusually committed young people like my friend and his family, I've concluded that there are some things we parents can do. They demand time and effort and will greatly impact our schedule and pocketbook, but I believe they can indeed significantly affect our children's destiny.

STRATEGIES FOR INSTILLING HOLY AMBITION

1. Prayer. From the moment we know that this child is conceived, prayer for him or her is the most sensible and significant step we can take. It is as important as the physical nurture we so willingly give. Pray for his future as well as his present, for his character as well as his health, for his future mate as well as his studies. Ask your parents and the child's godparents to pray for the long-term development of his life as well as the obvious current concerns.

Just recently I've been visiting with a young woman, newly arrived in our church and newly married and full of enthusiasm. She does not come from a home where faith is particularly important, but the girl is hungry for the truth of Christ—so eager and full of enthusiasm to know God. What's the reason for this holy ambition? Someone, some-where, perhaps a grandparent or a friend, has been praying for this young woman. It's the only way I can account for this as we have talked together, as I have puzzled over this and questioned her about it.

Pray for your child to have an unusual desire to know and serve God. Pray for him to be a person who can be a dif-ference-maker. Not everyone is called to leadership—that is a special gift some have and some don't have. But all Christians are called to make a difference for the sake of the kingdom. This ability begins with prayer.

2. Fellowship. Take whatever steps you can to help your child be a part of a vital extended Christian family.

This means a good church that is committed to a vibrant children's and youth ministry. It is incredibly tough to be faithful to Christ as a youth in our culture. Our children need the friendship of other Christian young people. The child who has good friends, and the opportunity to participate in a vibrant and exciting Christian group, week in and week out, will find it much easier to stand strong for Christ.

One of my daughters is involved in a Bible study group in our basement every Tuesday morning at 6:30. Led by the wife of our local Young Life leader, it has been a vitally important factor in Allison's Christian growth and stability. All five of our children are involved in similar activities. We don't force their involvement but we do encourage, and we do all we can to help the leaders out since they are helping us disciple our children.

As the children get older, it's important to use the summers to help them have formative experiences which will bring them into contact with a wide variety of Christian people, going to summer camps or houseparties, serving on short-term mission trips, counseling younger ones at Christian day camps, etc. *Expose them* to a great variety of exciting and challenging ministries.

Most parents of teens are concerned that their children get summer jobs and contribute toward their college funds, and as a result don't think very creatively about how best to use the summer vacation time to broaden the children's vision of the Christian life. There may be a way to do both at the same time. Our experience has been that spending some of the summertime in a broad range of Christian activities will give the children a valuable, stretching framework.

There may be very good reasons for wanting your child to earn money in the summer, but if it is to make it possible for him to have the latest stereo equipment and wear the big name-brand clothes, I seriously question it. The summers of a junior or senior high youth are among the most formative of their lives.

These experiences are reinforcing the nurture you are seeking to provide at home. It's a big mistake to think that you alone can give your children all the training and guidance in Christian living that they need. No Christian is to live in isolation. Your home shouldn't be the sole place where the child prays or learns from the Scriptures. We need one another, and there are incredible opportunities available.

3. Exposure to models. My parents were the first visionary Christians that I knew and were terrific models for me. Your own example as a growing Christian parent cannot be overemphasized. But your example may not be enough.

Most children need to be exposed to *many* different mature Christian men and women, and somewhere in the mix they meet a few whose example is so significant that the child's own personal vision for himself is powerfully affected. By God's grace, we can teach our own children much of what it means to be a Christian man or woman, and our impact on our children's lives is more significant than anyone else's. But look for ways to expose your child to more.

Read exciting stories to your young children of people of faith and vision. When they are older, buy good biographies for them to read on their own. I came along before the revisionists started tearing down the Founding Fathers, and the stories of courage, truthfulness, honor, and faith made a deep mark on me. Books like these are now becoming available again. If you read to your children when they are young, they are much more likely to become avid readers themselves.

There are also many exceptionally good videos now available that provide important stories and exemplary models for our children.

But more effective than these is exposure to flesh-and-blood people who are seeking to live their lives for Christ in a variety of ways. There are people like this in your own church, I expect. Have them over—help your children get to know them as you do. Keep the children with you as together you discuss some of the deeper, more challenging aspects of being a Christian today.

I doubt very seriously that I would have become a minister had I not had several rather special clergyman friends to look up to. I met them through my parents when I was young, through my older brother and my sisters as I became older, and then later met them on my own. But my vision of what God is calling me to be was as deeply influenced by the professor or horse trainer or headmaster or coach who was an adult Christian influence in my young life as it was by the clergymen I knew. Our vision for our own lives is shaped and molded by the influence of so many models.

4. Travel. A few years ago I took one of my children with me to Eastern and Southern Africa and to Israel. We stayed with missionary friends from our own church, with national Christian leaders and their friends as well. It was a learning time for me and my daughter, as we had one new experience after another. She will never forget the great variety of God's family which we encountered or the wonderfully diverse ways in which God worked in the lives of different people. Seeing the great needs in another part of the world and seeing that God's family is multinational, multicultural, and multiracial made a big impact on her. Getting away from her own familiar environment, being forced to trust God in new and sometimes threatening environments magnified her own sense of vision. Now as she anticipates entering college, she is much influenced in her thinking about her college major and career plans by the time spent in Africa.

If you travel as part of your work—or even if you take vacations—plan ahead some time to take a child with you and, as is possible, make arrangements to visit other Christian friends while you travel. Visit other churches, learn about ministries in other parts of the country, and talk together about these things as you travel.

5. Our example and relationship with our children. Surely as important as anything is *our* example and relationship with our children. Do they see us living our own lives in such a way as to serve God as fully as we can? Children are parent-watchers. They will imitate us in ways we do not imagine, and the importance we ourselves place on being Christ's men and women will be rather evident to them.

My two older brothers went into the same business as my father. He absolutely adored the field of merchandising—he was a faithful Christian all his life as well. But then when I was about sixteen (my two brothers were already grown by that time), he experienced a radical renewal in his own faith. He began to make significant changes in his own lifestyle and habits. I was watching. Business became less important, but encouraging business people to come to Christ and giving sacrificially to various ministries became paramount. Somehow I got the message and never even seriously considered business. Interestingly, my Dad seemed puzzled that I would go to seminary instead of following in his footsteps in the family business—he didn't realize that I was indeed following his footsteps in the way that made the most sense to me. I was getting a new message from him— "Serve God, make your life count for him."

Granted, many kids rebel and reject their parents' values, but this is usually temporary. Generally they come back to embrace what their parents embraced.

Perhaps as influential as anything are the experiences that we share from our own lives or experience together with our children, and the conversations that we have with our children as they are growing up. You can't just suddenly begin having deep conversations with your children when they become teenagers, but if you have habitually talked deeply and caringly with them about what is going on in your life and what is going on in their lives from the time they are quite small then this will continue to be the pattern during the years when they become older and their character is really being shaped through the major decisions that they have to make. We should especially share with them decisions that are demanding us to exercise our own faith and commitment to Christ so they can see his impact on our lives.

Families that don't make a priority of having at least one meal together daily miss out on a golden opportunity for lively, spirited, and meaningful discussion that can shape a child's thinking forever. Talk about each other's activities, trials, challenges, relationships, and plans. Talk about what is being studied in school, about what's happening in the community, the church, the neighborhood, the nation, and the world. Talk about questions that you have been grappling with.

Recently we needed a new automobile. Everything—new or used—that I priced was way out of the realm of our financial possibility. I was discouraged. Finally, one night I called my wife and all five children together for a family meeting. I shared with them my great frustration at not being able to provide a car for them. I had come to the limit of my faith and resources and needed their prayers. We prayed together that God would either show Dad how it would be possible to purchase an automobile, or that he would somehow provide one out of his own abundance. We even prayed that he would give us something safe and strong and secure. It was a memorable time of prayer.

A few days later I had a phone call from a local business-man. He said that he had heard that I needed an automobile. (I had shared my concern about an automobile with a friend in the church, who in turn had shared it with another, who in turn had apparently asked this businessman at a break-fast meeting if he knew of a good used car.) As it turned out, he had a late-model Volvo that had been bought by the company, paid for, and totally depreciated. It had now been replaced and was no longer needed by the company. It had all new equipment on it and was in excellent shape—safe, strong, secure. He sold it to me for one dollar.

Every time I get in this car now I'm overwhelmed at the mercy and care of God. All of our family together learned a fresh lesson of God's concern for even our most basic and functional needs. It is experiences like this that occur when we share together. The children come to see that God wants to be involved in every aspect of our lives. Because we experienced the lesson of faith together, our children will be able to apply it in their own lives.

6. Remind them of their destiny. A final suggestion comes from the biblical tradition of naming a child with a name that suggests something of his destiny or his personality. Samuel means "asked of God"; John means "gift of God"; Abraham means "Father of many"; Isaac means "laughter." Every time the child's name was called, it was a special reminder that God had his own purposes for the child.

We no longer follow this tradition but can learn from it. Without playing God in our child's life, we can still tell him of his gifts and encourage him over and over to believe that he can do this or be that with God's help. I'm not comfortable with telling a child she should be a doctor or a teacher or whatever, but we certainly ought to take every opportunity to let them know what special gifts we see in their own lives.

Telling your child in a strong, positive fashion that he is good with people, or a good organizer, that she is a leader or a good listener simply helps the child to develop a strong self image. When I was seven, I remember my mother bragging about my reading ability. She once made a tape of me reading a story. This said louder than words that "you are a good reader." I've enjoyed reading ever since.

Dream dreams with your child about his life, pray with him about his future. Carefully observe and study your child. If you do notice that your child really could become quite effective in this or that profession, tell him or her, "Honey, people listen to you, they are drawn to you," "Son, you really have an unusual ability to show compassion," "you have so many good ideas, I think you should run for class office—you can really have an impact in your school."

As you see their gifts, encourage them to put their gifts to work. Give the organizer an administrative job in the house; encourage the compassionate one to reach out to this or that needy person; gently push the leader to initiate this or that. Tell them what they are good at, and help them perceive how they can be a difference-maker in their own environment, and think with them, helping them learn what steps to take. Pray with them about these things.

It would be quite wrong, I believe, to decide in advance what career my child is going to pursue—this needs to be the child's decision as he or she seeks God's guidance in the coming years. But we can help them think realistically about their God-given strengths, talents, and spiritual gifts, and help them to enlarge their personal vision. To do any less is to deprive them of a parent's wisdom. They need to learn how to dream big dreams. And they will, if you show them how.

TWENTY-FIVE

Teaching Children about Sex

Barbara A. Stevenson

T HE WOMAN ON THE TELEPHONE was clearly distraught. She had just discovered that her two stepchildren, ages fifteen and seventeen, were sexually active. "What do we do?" she queried.

The problem she faces is one faced by countless parents today. With the steady decline of morals and the continued rise in teen pregnancy, many parents anticipate the adolescent years with a great sense of foreboding. Others deal with the problem by refusing to face it. "Not *our* child!" I've heard them say. "*Our* child would never do such a thing!" Wiser parents realize that Christian young people face the same temptations that are encountered by their non-Christian peers, and they long to prepare them for those temptations and teach them how to resist. "I don't want to ignore it like my parents did with me," a young mother confided recently. "I know the problems I got into!"

THE PARENTS' OWN ATTITUDES

Wanting to adequately prepare children by instilling Christian attitudes toward sex and being able to do so, however, are not at all the same thing. Many parents, while wanting desperately to do a good job in this area, have no pattern to follow and know neither when nor how to begin.

They are like the woman who came to me years ago when I was working as a school counselor. I had scheduled a film on menstruation for fifth and sixth-grade girls, and she was so relieved! "I've wanted to tell my daughter about it," she said, "but I didn't know how. My mother never told me anything. I just started my period one day, and I was so scared and so ashamed. I didn't want the same thing to happen to *my* daughter, but I didn't know what words to use to tell her!"

Many parents feel they don't have "the words" simply because their own training in such matters was woefully inadequate. They find it hard to teach what they were not taught. To make matters worse, their early knowledge was often obtained from faulty and inadequate sources. Perhaps it was a whispered word from a girlfriend, a magazine passed around among the boys, or mere biological facts presented in school without accompanying values and deep meanings—the mechanics without the beauty and sacredness of sex.

With many people, not only were early attitudes determined by the way in which their knowledge was gained, but their present approach to the subject of sex is still colored by those early associations or experiences. As I counsel women in this area, I find that they often bring into their adult lives carryovers from these childhood experiences. Sometimes their parents, having legitimate concern for their purity and safety, gave them dire warnings about misuse of their bodies and the dangers of sexual activity. They grew up thinking of sex as sinful, dirty, or frightening. When they married, somehow they were expected to accomplish a mental turnaround that never took place! Others were involved in sex play as little girls or heavy petting or promiscuity as teenagers, and the shame and guilt linger to spoil their present attitudes toward sex. Many times, it was something that was done to them, and the painful memories of molestation have not only left deep emotional scars, but often a deep revulsion for sex as well.

Certainly, every parent needs to examine personal attitudes toward sex and sexuality and compare them with God's attitudes as revealed in his Word. Does the parent see sex as God sees it? The Bible speaks of sex as pure, clean, pleasurable, satisfying, and fulfilling, a precious gift to be enjoyed by husband and wife. Does the parent view the body as God's creation, and is there, then, a deep appreciation and respect for the entire body and its functions? While some parents may need only a slight adjustment to bring their attitudes into line with God's attitudes, others need a complete overhaul. They need to be open and honest with God, freely confessing their wrong attitudes and asking him to cleanse or change those attitudes. Then they can fully appreciate both his gift of sex and their sexuality the way he intended. For some parents, problems may be so severe that professional help is needed and should be sought.

In any case, putting away childish carryovers and self-imposed inhibitions and developing a biblical attitude toward sex and sexuality will free a couple to *pass on* this attitude to their children. They can begin sex education when a child is born by the loving attitudes they show toward each other and the loving, wholesome attitudes they demonstrate to the child. The teaching that a child receives concerning sexuality is not confined to a "facts-of-life" discussion at puberty. Indeed, it begins with the child's earliest contact with the parents, and continues as long as the child is in the home. Concerned parents, therefore, take every opportunity to help the child develop a wholesome, balanced attitude toward his or her own sexuality, and, as the child grows, a wholesome, balanced attitude toward sex.

TEACHING THE YOUNG CHILD

The Infant. The way a baby is held close and cuddled, the tender, gentle manner in which the baby is bathed, the positive attitude displayed by a parent changing a soiled diaper (rather than an attitude of cringing displeasure), all go together to form the child's early attitudes toward his or her own body. Baths also present an excellent opportunity to teach small children the names of body parts and respect for those parts. Even little ones pick up quickly on embarrassment or avoidance on the part of a parent, but if the parent bathes each part of the body with equal care and acceptance, the child learns to accept the body as good and worthy of respect. As parents wash and dry each part, they can casually and naturally teach correct names for those parts, including the child's sex organs. If the parent is unsure of correct terms or uncomfortable using them, then the parent ought to become familiar with them and practice using them with the child.

Biological differences can also be taught in a natural, casual manner when children are quite young. A small sister and brother can be bathed together, with the attending parent alert to matter-of-factly answer any questions that may arise concerning anatomical differences. The parent can explain that God made little boys to be daddies and little girls to be mommies, that is why he has a penis and she has a vagina. A small child watching a parent change the diaper of baby brother or sister may also ask questions which the parent can answer to help the child understand the differences early on. If no questions are forthcoming, the parent can casually point out the differences. One three-year-old, watching her mother bathe her baby brother, questioned, "When he grows up, will he be nice like I am?" The mother was puzzled for a moment, then realized that the little girl had watched as the baby's umbilical cord had dried up and dropped off and that she evidently expected the rest of his anatomy to follow suit! The incident gave the mother needed opportunity to explain to her some of the obvious differences between boys and girls!

An expected baby in the family affords a good opportunity to teach some of the marvelous truths about conception and birth. Even the smallest of children will be thrilled to feel the baby kicking in Mommy's growing stomach. One young couple told their two-and-one-half-year-old about the expected arrival early in the pregnancy, then kept him updated on the current size of the baby. They showed him how to position his hands to indicate how big, and let the child view the ultrasound toward the end of the pregnancy. What a marvelous introduction to the miracle of life!

The Preschooler. Parents of preschoolers need to seize opportunities to expose them to the simple lessons afforded in nature regarding life, sexuality, and reproduction. The parent can design occasions for the child to observe caterpillars, butterflies, tadpoles, frogs, birds' eggs, and other such wonders of nature. Together they can plant seeds and care for struggling seedlings, and they can share the miracle of birth as a pet hamster, cat, or dog bears its young. In all this, the child is being educated in God's truth, and, as the parent expresses wonder and delight in these experiences and emphasizes how God planned it all; the child can develop an appreciation for that plan and form healthy, positive attitudes toward sexuality and reproduction.

The Older Child. Books provide another tool which should not be overlooked in guiding children toward a Christian view of sex. Young children delight in having parents read to them. Some older children enjoy sharing books with parents while others prefer to read on their own. The young mother mentioned before, who did not want to ignore the subject of sex as her parents had done, spent a good deal of time browsing in Christian bookstores and talking with Christian counselors and educators. Finally she compiled a list of books which she could read for herself and share with her children. She found books helpful in stimulating thinking and promoting discussion on the part of her school-age son and daughter.

Another way for parents to share their understanding and promote good discussions with children as they grow is for the family to visit a science museum to view models of the developing baby in the mother's uterus. Together they can marvel at the wonder of God's plan.

ANSWERING DIFFICULT QUESTIONS

As the questions come, whether the child is three or thirteen, they need to be answered simply and honestly. The answers, of course, must differ according to the age and level of understanding of the child. Parents need to make sure they completely understand the question so that they can answer what has been asked. "Mom, where did I come from?" More than one parent has stumbled through an ill-prepared, all-inclusive answer about sperm and egg only to discover that the child was asking a completely different question! "Well, Billy said he came from Detroit, and I didn't know where I came from."

Parents should also use terminology which the child can understand and only give as much information as the child is capable of comprehending. The young child who questions how the baby gets out of mommy's tummy can be told that God has made a special opening for the baby to come out. When the child wants to know where the opening is, the parent can simply explain that the opening is between mommy's legs, but that it has nothing to do with going to the bathroom, that God has given mommy three openings, and that one of these is for the baby. If the child asks how the baby began to grow in mommy's tummy, the parent can reply that the baby began from a tiny egg from the mother and a tiny sperm from the father. Later, when the child begins to ask questions about how the sperm from the daddy got into the mommy, a simple answer that the daddy put it there will usually suffice. As the child matures and asks further questions, the parent can explain that God made the daddy and mommy so that they can join together at special times, that he made the daddy's penis so that it can fit perfectly into the mommy's vagina, and that is how the daddy places the sperm in the mommy so that they can have a baby to love.

Parents need to take care to answer questions in a casual but sincere manner that leaves the door open for further questions. If the child's time is poor and questions are asked at inopportune times (as they often are!), the parent can give a brief answer and then come back to the question later when the timing is more appropriate. The important thing is that the child regards the parent as ready and willing to answer. One woman reported the vivid memory of asking her mother about a pregnant neighbor. She recalls being seven or eight at the time and she remembers innocently inquiring why the lady's tummy was so large. Her mother replied that the lady was expecting a baby, but there was something about the look on her mother's face or her tone of voice that made the child think she had done a bad thing in asking. She never asked another question, and she went through her teen years picking up information from the streets when she desperately needed it from her mother!

In addition to giving children correct, God-centered information early—before some street-wise classmate shares faulty information with them—it is important for parents to protect their children from negative influences as much as is within their power. Among other things, this means carefully monitoring the TV programs which come into the home and being aware of what is going on when children are at play. Unless they are certain that the parents of playmates hold to the same standards and exert the same supervision, then they need to make sure the children play at home and invite their friends there. One mother learned this the hard way, when she discovered that the little neighbor girls with whom her son played were allowed to play in the nude!

PREPARING FOR PUBERTY

As children near puberty, parents need to make every effort to prepare them for the changes that will be taking place, both physically and emotionally. Dr. James Dobson has written a book and prepared a set of tapes, *Preparing for Adolescence,* which are designed to aid the parent and child in addressing the changes that lie ahead. If a parent has made sex education an ongoing process as the child has grown, it will not be difficult to address the subject now. If not, this is an excellent time and way to let the child know that the parent is interested and wants to help. A friend of mine decided to take her daughter to the beach for the weekend so that the two of them could have a time to themselves. They played Dr. Dobson's tapes and discussed each in depth. They talked about the pressures that the girl would face in dating and how she could handle those pressures. At the end of the weekend, my friend gave her daughter a little gold heart with a keyhole in it and a tiny key attached. Engraved on the heart was, "he who holds the key can unlock my heart." As they talked about the importance of purity and waiting until marriage for sex, the mother challenged her daughter to save herself for her husband and to present him with the little key on her wedding night! It was a meaningful time for both mother and daughter, one that brought them closer together and helped the daughter determine to keep her standards high!

Having a parent show such concern and interest makes a difference in a young person's life. One young woman told me how her father had taken her out for a "date." While they ate their hamburgers and french fries, they talked about choosing friends, what to look for in a boy, how to set life goals, and so on. As she grew into her teen years, she not only knew what character qualities to look for in a young man, but she also knew how to plan her dates so that her conduct would remain chaste!

SUPPORTING TEENAGERS

Teenagers need such closeness with their parents! They need to know that they can talk to them about the sexual pressures they face, and that their parents are confident that they have the courage and determination to withstand those pressures. Above all, they need to regard their bodies as temples of the Holy Spirit and have an inner desire to keep their bodies pure and clean. The example of parents in this area is crucial! The father who demands modest dress and behavior from his daughter, yet lets his eyes follow every scantily-clad woman who passes by, or the mother who expects purity in her children but who is personally attracted to the bed-hopping antics of the TV soaps, can expect young people to emulate what they have seen, not what they have heard!

But parents who make every effort to lead their children to the Lord early, who give attention to developing a wholesome, God-centered attitude toward sex and sexuality, and who, by example, demonstrate lives lived in purity and obedience to God's commands, are parents who will ultimately succeed in seeing their children evidence the same Christian view of sex that has been lived before them.

TWENTY-SIX

Teaching Teens to Say "No"

Tim Stafford

F OR THE LAST FIFTEEN YEARS I have written a monthly magazine column, answering kids' questions about love, sex, and dating. There are very few teenage questions I haven't answered in print at least five times. Consequently I don't feel particularly nervous discussing sex with teenagers. I'm not embarrassed by the subject, and I don't fear being stumped.

An event is coming, though, that scares me greatly. Very soon my daughter Katie will celebrate her thirteenth birthday. More than most parents, I am aware of the frighteningly sex-saturated world she will struggle with.

Even so, it will not be easy to discuss with her the same beliefs I have shared with millions of other kids. When you are talking to your own child, sex is a difficult subject.

That is why so few parents really talk about it. Very few kids get more than a nervous "facts-of-life" lecture from their parents—if they even get that. It's uncomfortable for parents, and for kids, too.

Yet parents are often the only ones likely to have a say in favor of the Christian view of sex. Society doesn't believe in it. The media undermines it.

Public schools offer, at most, a weak-kneed encourage-ment to "be responsible." Church groups are often too skittish to offer any in-depth discussion. If kids don't get a Christian view of sex from their parents, they often just won't get it.

Why do teenage kids, even Christian kids, become sexually active? For the most part, because they believe it is right. Most American teenagers believe sex is appropriate "if you love each other."

Your teenage son or daughter will eventually, almost certainly, fall in love. Those are the circumstances under which most teenagers first become sexually involved—under the sway of intense romantic emotions.

What can you say to help them see that sex "if we love each other" is a *second-best* choice? They do not need warnings to "be careful." They need a philosophy of sex. And it's not something that only parents can do; church youth leaders can also effectively address some of these topics.

Here are some pointers:

1. Avoid making negative health consequences your major emphasis. Herpes, chlamydia, AIDS, and pregnancy are risks of premarital sex, and I would certainly speak of them. But kids are rarely persuaded by them. Teenagers just don't believe anything can hurt them. Also, they can (and will) argue that using condoms would solve these problems. Then would premarital sex be all right?

2. Avoid giving the impression that sex is unpleasant or dirty, or that premarital sex always brings consuming guilt. Your kids probably know more people who've re-cently surrendered their virginity than you do. At any rate, Robert Coles and Geoffrey Stokes in their study, *Sex and the American Teenager,* found that kids who say their parents

taught that sex is "not healthy and normal" are para-
doxically more likely than others to engage in premarital
sex.

**3. Emphasize that there is no such thing as sexual exper-
imentation.** When you go to bed with someone, you give a
part of yourself to him or to her. You will never lose the
memories of those moments. If you marry someone else
someday, you will take the ghost of that "first partner" with
you on your honeymoon.

Furthermore, you cannot try sex out to see if you like it.
Couples who have sexual relations usually cannot stop.
Surveys indicate that they usually will go on to a series of
other partners.

**4. Emphasize that if you want to know whether a relation-
ship is "true love," there is only one reliable test.** Are you
both ready and willing to have a wedding ceremony—to
declare your commitment in front of family, friends, and
God? To live together, legally tied together, sharing everything?

If you're not ready for that heady step, you can't be very
sure that your love will last. Weddings aren't guaranteed,
but they do provide the best test ever designed for
separating big talkers from the truly committed.

**5. Emphasize that sexual purity matters tremendously to
you.** I have known parents who communicate quite clearly
the importance of hard work, of a productive career, of
honesty. But perhaps because of embarrassment, they give
the impression that good sexual behavior is optional.

Teenagers need to know that the Christian view of sex is
central to their parents' ambitions for them. The thought
that "this is extremely important to my parents" can carry
them a long distance, even when they're not sure just what
they think themselves.

Sex education of this kind must start early. The seeds are planted in the preteen years. A lot of parents, I believe, start thinking seriously about discussing sex when their kids turn thirteen and get around to it (if they get around to it at all) at about fifteen or sixteen. They just can't imagine anything happening before then.

If surveys are true, however, just as many kids are introduced to sexual intercourse at age thirteen as at sixteen, seventeen, or eighteen. By the late teens, many of them have made up their minds.

If you find it hard to say all you want to say, all is not lost. Use books and magazines. Kids may not read much, but they *will* read about sex. Choose literature that says what you want to communicate, and pass it on. Write a note to accompany the gift, spelling out why you're giving it and making the way open for further conversation.

This is not a substitute for personal involvement. But it can make communication a lot easier.

Another option is to "trade" responsibilities with other parents or with youth workers. A Kenyan psychiatrist, Samuel Gatere, says that in his own traditional society, grandparents or family friends were designated to provide sex education. Talking about sex with their own children was considered too sensitive. Gatere suggests that modern parents agree to help each other out.

The strongest predictor of whether teenagers will have sexual intercourse, according to Coles and Stokes, is whether or not they are influenced by religion. A 1986 Lou Harris poll showed a similar difference between teenagers who attended church often and those who attended seldom. Teenagers who have responded to God are less likely than others to engage in sexual intercourse.

We're asking kids to swim against the stream. Very few kids will be able to do so without the internal strength that comes from faith in God. You can't force that on your kids.

But you can make sure they get every opportunity to learn about it.

Research also indicates that a teenager's lifestyle makes a difference. For instance, kids who drink alcohol are far more likely to be involved in premarital sex than those who don't. Frequent marijuana use also has an effect. Kids who do well in school, who have plans for a good education, are much less likely to be sexually involved.

A philosophy of sex cannot simply be said; it must be lived. Indeed, Coles and Stokes found that teenagers from divorced families are about twice as likely to engage in premarital sex as kids whose parents are still together. If your children see the beauty of a Christian marriage, they will want it. If they don't admire what you show them, no amount of talking will affect them.

Sometimes parents need to "show off" their joy in marriage. Counselor Walter Trobisch always made a point of kissing his wife first when he came home, before greeting his children. One couple I know, when going out for the evening, tells their young children they are looking forward to being romantic, complete with hugging and kissing. The kids say, "Yuck," but they are getting the idea that marriage is fun.

Most teenagers long for love and intimacy more than they long for sex. If they experience it in their family life, they'll be a lot less frantic in their search for it in romance with their peers.

The adult world, filled with brokenness and embittered people, can look pretty awful to a kid. Christian parents need to model something better, give their children hope that marriage is worth waiting for. (Divorced or widowed parents need to make sure healthy, intact families enter their children's lives.) Otherwise, teenagers will grab for whatever wisps of intimacy they can find.

Statistics on teenage sexuality are scary. Kids seem to live in a world out of control. But the temptations are not terribly different from those we and our parents and grandparents experienced. It's just that most kids no longer have the benefit of parents (and a society) urging them to keep their urges under control.

Parents and youth leaders can help our kids by communicating a Christian philosophy of sex, by creating a strong and intimate family where teenagers find the love they crave, and by making clear what we expect of them.

TWENTY-SEVEN

What Parents Can Do about Drugs and Alcohol

Stephen Arterburn

I F YOU ARE A "NORMAL" CHRISTIAN PARENT, you probably believe that raising a child in a Christian home is the best defense against drugs and alcohol. You pray for your children and encourage them to do their best. You teach your kids to honor God in all they do and make sure they know doing drugs does not fit in that category. And if you are like most Christian parents, you trust that doing these things will be enough.

"It won't happen to us" is woven into every thought concerning your children and drugs. Sadly, evidence does not support the beliefs of the "normal" Christian parent. Many discover this mistake only after a child has been found with drugs, arrested for drunk driving, or is already the victim of a deadly addiction.

Take the case of a devoted Christian couple who called me about the husband's brother. The husband knew his brother was an alcoholic and was also raising two alcoholic sons. He was concerned for the entire family, having watched them all battle each other as the vise of addiction clamped harder and harder. Together, we made plans to intervene in the whole family. As we developed a strategy, I questioned the husband about others who would be involved in the intervention process. Discovering that the husband had two sons, I asked him questions regarding their behavior. I was assured that neither was involved in drugs. Both sons were "strong athletes with high morals and good discipline," the father stated confidently. He had no need to focus on the boys, it was his brother and nephews that he wanted to help. Together we did help his brother and nephews. But our efforts should have been directed closer to home.

The man's wife contacted me a few weeks later. It was the oldest son that presented her with one of the greatest shocks of parenthood. He had left a small pipe in a jacket. She knew that it was some type of drug paraphernalia. Rather than confront the son, she called me for advice. I told her that no matter what the boy said once she confronted him, she was only seeing the tip of the iceberg. The boy's goal has been to hide and cover up. She had only seen one of hundreds of pieces of evidence that would lead to the conclusion: the boy was a drug addict.

The mother left me and confronted her son with the pipe. Caught with the evidence, he knew outright denial would not work. So he admitted to an occasional "harmless" smoke of marijuana. He said he had done it for several years, and that it had never been a problem. This admission led the mother to conduct an investigation through her son's friends, her other son, and the parents of her son's friends. She discovered that she was the last to know just how serious a problem her son had. Each discussion and interview deepened her sadness as she discovered her son was a chemical gourmet. Under her roof, living as a wonderful Christian athlete, was a drug addict, clever enough to keep the problem completely hidden for years. A drug addict that looked and talked like all the other Christian kids in the church youth group.

This case is not unusual. It is very common for Christian parents to be caught up in helping others while someone close is in need of help. Christian parents are easily fooled, because they want to believe the best about their kids. And their kids look so good! But in Christian homes, the *best* Christian homes, kids are drinking and doing drugs. This is supported by some research Jim Burns and I discovered while writing the book *Drug-Proof Your Kids*. The average church-going child, before graduating from high school will have:

- an 85 percent chance of experimenting with alcohol
- a 57 percent chance of trying an illicit drug
- a 33 percent chance of smoking marijuana occasionally
- a 25 percent chance of smoking marijuana regularly
- a 17 percent chance of trying cocaine or crack.[1]

The survey—taken in 1987 before the epidemic of crack-cocaine thoroughly infiltrated both urban and rural America—is a conservative assessment of the level of drug and alcohol involvement among the best kids. It proves that it is not enough to raise a child in a Christian home. It takes more than that to combat the problem, and parents are the only ones who can provide the needed action to produce drug-proof kids.

The following information provides the concrete steps that Christian parents must take to protect their children from drugs. There is no greater threat to a child's faith than drugs. Addiction will take a child's faith and Christian values and rip them out of the child's heart. Addiction will leave a child alienated from God, parents, and anything else that stands in the way of "fixing" the craving for an altered mood or a quick high. Keeping your kids Christian must involve a plan that fights drug and alcohol use, heading off the addiction process before its claws have pierced the surface of your child's soul.

The steps that follow are your greatest hope for producing

a drug-free child. But these steps do not stand alone; they must serve as an adjunct to the other parenting principles contained within the other chapters. The other areas form the foundation of Christian principles. They are the core of a drug-proof plan from which these principles extend. Without the solid core, these will do no better than other secular approaches that have failed to help parents and kids. Combined with the foundation of Christian parenting, they provide the hope that thousands have failed to find outside of Christ and the church.

STEP ONE: SELF-EXAMINATION

This is the most difficult step to take in a plan to produce a drug-free child. The degree of difficulty provides the reason so few do it and so many fail with their kids. The fact remains, you cannot prevent your child from becoming involved in the drugs of his or her culture if you are involved with the drugs of your culture. It just doesn't compute when a half-drunk parent sipping a cocktail discusses problem-drinking and drugs with a child. The incongruity is not missed by the child. Seeing a parent abuse a substance will either lead the child to follow the same example, or to try to drink or use drugs the "correct" way. Stories abound in treatment of kids who had an alcoholic parent and so tried to outdrink their parents. "I swore I would never be like my father," is a common battle cry of cloned children of alcoholics seeking treatment for their own alcoholism. To be effective in this battle you cannot start with your kids, you must start with yourself.

I have an acquaintance whose son has had a drug problem since the age of sixteen. They have tried counseling, outpatient treatment, inpatient treatment, prayer, and just about everything else you could do but one thing. They have not given up their own drinking, which is excessive. I know that once the decision is made by the parents to stop, the boy will follow. Until they decide to quit, their efforts are futile.

Of course, this is an unpopular position for many who read this. I hear parents say things like, "I have to live my life, and my children have choices to make on their own. I do not control their choices." The old "do as I say, and not as I do" philosophy and practice has never worked, and it certainly won't work with alcohol and drugs. Since your children were very small they have been playing a game called "follow the leader." No one had to teach it to them. They were born with an instinctive ability to play it. No matter what their age, they continue to play that game. The leaders they are following include you. Your example in relation to the drugs of your culture will always be more powerful than your explanation of the drugs of their culture.

A parent totally committed to setting the best example for kids will examine all of his or her behaviors of excess. Ask yourself, "Is food a drug? Is work an escape? Is there something controlling you?" If the answer is yes, the greatest gift you can give your children is your own recovery. Your courage to finally say "no" may be the perfect example in your child's battle to say "no." Your willingness to examine yourself could be the motivation for your child to refuse to go the way of the crowd. Taking action on your own problem is the greatest tool you can use to combat problems with your problem. Before you take action, you must take a look at yourself and the example you set. Although painful, the first step of self-examination will be productive for you and your child.

STEP TWO: EDUCATION

This step is too often left to someone else. Although drugs and alcohol will kill more of our children and derail more from the tracks of greatness, few parents will take the time to read a book or see a film on how to educate a child about alcohol and drugs. If your attitude is "they teach them that stuff at school," you may be surprised at what they do teach. Many drug education programs are not focused on abstinence. Their goal is to produce kids who know how to drink responsibly. Some even teach responsible drug use from a view of marijuana in moderation being a harmless recreational drug. Often this material has been developed by those who used drugs in the sixties and seventies and became confused adults in the eighties. You cannot entrust your child to someone else, when you do not know the focus of the information or its contents. School programs have not delivered the desired results because of their valueless foundation and confused messages to kids.

A *Wall Street Journal* reporter went to Bainbridge High School in Washington to interview kids and teachers about the drug program there. One of those interviewed said, "Drugs are as plentiful as potato chips." School officials admitted the program was a failure. As many as seventy percent of the students used alcohol or drugs weekly.[2] This may not be alarming to you, but it probably affects your children. You see, Bainbridge High School's drug education program was implemented twelve years ago. It has served as a model for school systems across America. Bainbridge High School is a glaring example of our need to take responsibility for our children, rather than delegate vital issues to others. The issue of drug education must not be passed on to others.

To educate your child, start young and keep it simple. A preschooler should be told of "magic pills" that people might try to hand out. Their harmful effects can be summarized as "bad for you." Tell your children not to chew, eat, or swallow anything given to them unless they have your okay. This simple discussion begins the process of your growing involvement with your child and drugs. Start early to win the credibility battle, and continue to win it as you learn more and present more information as the child grows older. By the sixth grade you should have discussed all of the major drugs including why people take them, what effects they have and how they harm people. This information is detailed in *Drug-Proof Your Kids*.[3] It can also be obtained at a local library or from the Council on Alcohol and Drug Abuse.

Taking the time to learn the basic facts about drugs and presenting them to your child opens communication surrounding this difficult subject. It also shows the child of your care and concern. You establish yourself as a credible source rather than a naive, easily fooled parent. This process makes you an active participant in your child's life. While other parents ignore the problem or address it from some ill-advised tangent, you tackle the problem with accurate information. This proactive approach to drug education is the only approach that will work for you and your child. Failing to be the resource for drug information is a mistake too many parents have made.

STEP THREE: PREVENTION

A step beyond educating your child with facts is implementing prevention techniques that motivate your child to refuse to participate in drug or alcohol use. Telling a child not to drink because of the possibility of cirrhosis of the liver at age sixty-five will do nothing to assist the child in the decision process of whether or not to use. Long-term consequences mean little or nothing to kids. Short-term consequences mean a lot to a child. Combined with short-term rewards, they constitute the prevention plan that motivates a good decision.

A seventeen-year-old will think little of the dangers of drinking and driving. Death is an unfathomable consequence to the immortal mindset of an adolescent. Loss of life is no deterrent. But loss of a license is. Many states now take away a driver's license one year for each drug or alcohol-related offense. A parent should do no less. Sit down with the child at age fifteen, sixteen, or seventeen and ask him or her to imagine walking during the entirety of his or her senior year. Tell the child that if you discover alcohol or drug use, you will tear up his driver's license. This will have an effect. This will get the child's attention. Then the child, when offered alcohol or drugs can say, "I'd love to, but my crazy parents will not let me drive if they find out."

A similar technique can be used at other ages. Ask an eighth grader to imagine going a full year without using the telephone. You will have his or her attention. Most eighth graders cannot imagine one day without the telephone. Tell the child that if alcohol or drug use is discovered, his freshman year of high school will be one without phone privileges. Explain what it is like to be cut off from the rest of the world from 6:00 P.M. until 8:00 A.M. the next day. Help the child feel the consequence. Then when confronted with the temptation to use the child can explain, "Drugs might be fun, but I would never be able to use the phone again because of my 'crazy' parents."

To balance the restrictions for poor choices, there should be some rewards for good choices. Find what is meaningful to the child and hold it out as a reward for staying clean. Draw up a contract that states what will happen if the child makes the decision to overcome peer pressure. The reward must fit your own economic level, but some rewards parents have used are the following: a trip to a special place with a friend, a car for college or financial support for college. You must develop the reward from your child's own desires and your abilities. This reward should be something far above what your child would normally expect from you. In this drug-infested culture, you are expecting something far above what most parents will experience in a child. It will be worth the sacrifice you make to provide something special for special behavior.

Some parents believe that holding up a reward for behavior expected of any Christian child is setting an undesirable precedent. Their belief is that a child should make decisions for reasons other than material gain or tangible rewards. I agree that there are many better reasons to say "no" to drugs than a trip or a driver's license. But we must deal with kids where they are. We must relate to them in areas that they feel are important. We cannot graft our maturity onto them. This approach of rewards and restrictions is not a "cure-all." It does provide an important piece of the prevention plan. Without this piece, the rest of the plan would be greatly weakened. Education merely informs, prevention is the step that provides added incentive and motivation to say no. As an involved parent, you will find many other ways to add to the desire within the child to say no and remain drug-free.

STEP FOUR: IDENTIFICATION

The goal of any credible plan should be total abstinence on the part of the adolescent. If a child makes it to age eighteen without using drugs, the chances of starting after that are almost nonexistent. No plan will be one hundred percent successful for every child in this abstinence goal. If a child does use, there is an important next step. The sooner the parent takes this step, the less likely experimentation will become regular use or regular use become addiction. This next step is identifying drug use as soon as it starts. This is not always easy, but if you are involved with your child, you will know what is normal adolescent adjustment and what is more strange and bizarre, indicating drug involvement.

To assist you in this identification process, I have provided the following list of indicators to look for in a child. If you are not looking, you will not find them. You should not become a gestapo or KGB agent in your observation technique. You should increase your level of awareness so that you can assist the child in dealing with the problem if it occurs. Here are the most common indicators of a drug problem:

1. Paraphernalia found in the bedroom: strange vials, small bags, mirrors, pipes, tubes, razor blades, cigarette papers, butane lighters, scales, matches.
2. Possession of large amounts of money (may indicate your child uses and sells to other kids).
3. Needle marks on the arms, or clothing that prevents you from seeing the arms.
4. Valuables disappearing from your home.
5. Arrests due to alcohol or drug-related incidents.
6. Repeatedly blood-shot eyes.
7. Dilated or pinpoint pupils.
8. Puffy or droopy eyelids that partially hang over the iris.
9. Mention of suicide or a suicide attempt.
10. Disappearance or dilution of bottles in the liquor cabinet.
11. Time spent with kids you know use alcohol and drugs.
12. Medicine disappearing from the medicine cabinet.
13. Defending peers' right to use drugs or alcohol.

Sometimes symptoms can reflect another problem such as an eating disorder or depression. In that case the parent still needs to act on the information and solve the problem. The following list are symptoms that are less drug specific than the ones above, but, in combination with other symptoms, should cause a parent to act.

1. Deep depression accompanied by hours of extra sleep.
2. Extreme withdrawal from the family.
3. Increased, unexplained absenteeism from school.
4. Little or no involvement in church activities.

5. Increase in mysterious phone calls that produce a frantic reaction.
6. Starting cigarette smoking.
7. Extreme weight loss or gain.
8. Appearance of new friends, older than your child.
9. Expulsion from school.
10. Rebellious and argumentative behavior.
11. Listening to heavy metal rock music with pro-drug songs.
12. Acting disconnected or "spacey."
13. Physically hurting younger siblings.
14. Attempting to change the subject or skirt the issue when asked about drug or alcohol use.
15. Changing the word "party" from a noun to a verb.
16. Discussing times in the future when he or she will be able to drink normally.

A child free of drugs and alcohol will not normally be exhibiting symptoms from either of the above lists. If your child starts to show these signs and symptoms, even one or two, you should begin to suspect that a problem exists. Once you verify that there is a problem, you need to move to the next step in the plan. It is the step that requires immediate but well-planned action.

STEP FIVE: INTERVENTION

The knowledge of drug use throws many parents into a paralytic frenzy. They worry, fret, and dwell over the problem, but they do nothing to help change it. Some will do worse and deny what they see or ignore it, hoping it will go away. Others will try to pray it away or hope the child will grow out of this "stage" or phase. Of all of those options, prayer is the only one that helps. But prayer must be accompanied by action. The action needed is intervention.

Upon discovering evidence of drug use, most parents feel betrayed, a sense of failure, and intense anger. It is easy to react in a damaging way, confronting them with all of your emotional forces turned on the "rage level." This will not help. It will only force the child to go further underground with the problem. The process of intervention provides a forum for that confrontation that leads to the greatest chance for change. If you have discovered drugs or alcohol you should contact a local treatment center or agency that will help you intervene.

In an intervention, a parent gathers together, with the help of a counselor, people who know of the child's involvement with alcohol and drugs. These people include other parents who have seen the child use, teachers with evidence of classes missed or alcohol on the breath, a youth pastor or youth worker, friends of your child, and others. These people are often more aware of the problem than you are. You as a parent are usually the last to know, and what you do know is only the tip of the iceberg. Once you have found these people who can help, the intervention counselor will bring you together to prepare for the intervention.

The preparation for the intervention involves accumulating data that is specifically related to the alcohol and drug use of your child. The intervention counselor will have each person write out the specific details of the incident in which drugs or alcohol intake was observed. This will provide data as to the amount witnessed, frequency of use, and the child's behavior under the influence. Each participant will also state how he or she felt while watching the adolescent use. If a member of this intervention team does not have specific firsthand data, that person should not participate in the intervention. When all data is accumulated, a treatment resource selected, consequences for not seeking help agreed upon, and the actual intervention rehearsed, the intervention will be scheduled at a time when the adolescent is least likely to be under the influence of drugs or alcohol.

At the intervention, the child will be asked to listen to the participants present evidence of a growing problem. Each person will present the data, expressing what happened, the feelings surrounding the event, and the desire for change. A typical presentation would include comments like the following:

"Bobby, you know I love you and care about you greatly. But I am concerned about your drinking. When you came home last Friday at 2:00 A.M. you smelled of alcohol. Your eyes were bloodshot and in the middle of the night you were throwing up. On your way to your room you knocked over a lamp. When I went out to your car there were three empty beer cans. I cannot let you go on like this. I love you enough to help you help yourself. I want you to get treatment for your problem."

After each person has presented the data, one of the parents tells the child he or she must go into treatment, see a counselor, attend Alcoholics Anonymous, or participate in whatever treatment was previously selected. If the child agrees, then he or she should be taken to the resource for help immediately. If there is reluctance, the consequences must be spelled out in detail. These consequences are to be considered carefully beforehand with the counselor. These include moving out of the house, lack of financial support for college, and other difficult changes that force the child to realize the game is over. The parents must be willing to follow through on these, otherwise the intervention will be a failure. Many parents have drug users in their homes because they are not willing to follow through with this act of tough love.

The intervention is a powerful tool for change. It is the best form of confrontation in difficult cases. Not every case requires this. I was contacted by a couple whose son needed help. After discussing the problem, I felt they would do best to confront the child without me or anyone else present. They were willing to ask him to leave if he did not comply with their wishes. When they confronted him, rather than seek treatment, he chose to move out. Fortunately, after spending one night with a friend, that friend told him to go back home and get help. He did, and the parents are grateful they were willing to do the hard thing. Whether it is in a formal or informal intervention, you must come to the point of not being willing to be manipulated by the child. You must believe that forcing your child to decide between drugs and you may result in the child choosing drugs. This is a better alternative than allowing your child to use drugs with you being the major supplier. When you provide the comfortable setting of food and shelter, you are the chief enabler of a drug problem. Tough love is never easy, but it is a key element to a successful intervention and the arrest of a growing addiction or dependency.

STEP SIX: TREATMENT

Intervention, when successful, leads to treatment of the problem. Treatment can come in many forms. Attending Alcoholics Anonymous and "working" the twelve steps of that program is a form of treatment. Individual and family counseling are also treatments for addiction. There are also outpatient centers that provide a structured program for kids. My bias is for inpatient treatment, which we operate at New Life Treatment Centers. I prefer this treatment mode, because it occurs in a setting where quality control is monitored regularly. It allows the child to be separated from negative peer pressure and the family. It is an environment that allows for a "time-out" to evaluate decisions and behaviors and receive support for a new life free of drugs. When inpatient treatment is done properly, it is the best resource for the child and family. Since it involves all of the elements of the other treatment modalities: counseling, recovery groups, peer counseling, and outpatient aftercare, it is the most comprehensive resource available.

Parents should approach all treatment resources with caution. The Christian parent should especially be aware of differing philosophical approaches within a treatment center. Now more than ever, the New Age tenets are being incorporated within lectures and meditation time. An unknowing parent could be responsible for introducing a child to a totally secular outlook, or even to New Age religion. This problem is the motivation for New Life Treatment Centers, where traditional conservative Christian values are supported and taught. The counselors are Christians who are dedicated to upholding the power of Christ as the central force of recovery. We are not the only Christian treatment resource. With us and others like us, there is no reason to send a child to a non-Christian resource, if you need assistance.

One final note on treatment. For it to be effective, it must include a comprehensive program to treat the entire family. Kids do not become sick in a vacuum. They take the entire family with them through the progression of addiction. Just as the child does not get sick in isolation, he or she cannot get well in isolation. Returning a child to a troubled family will only produce temporary results. The child is sure to relapse without a major restructure of the family system. A quality treatment center will insure that each family member obtains the needed attention to provide an opportunity for everyone to be involved in recovery.

STEP SEVEN: SUPPORTIVE FOLLOW-UP

There is no quick-fix or cure-all that will work to eradicate addiction in an instant. Recovery is a process that takes time. Support for the process is a vital final step to free your child from addiction. At the heart of this support must be genuine forgiveness of the child. Often parents resent the child for not living up to expectations, or for failing to fulfill the dreams of the parent. With this resentment submerged just below the surface, the child is able to sense the parent's true feelings. These destructive emotions sabotage the child's recovery. The child feels total rejection sometimes expressed as, "My parents did not like me using, now they don't like me clean and sober." Feeling the despair of not being able to please, the child resorts to old friends and pressures, finally succumbing to the temptation to use again. Whatever you do, rid yourself of every shred of bitterness toward a recovering child. In its place, provide the support needed for a strong recovery.

CONCLUSION

No one is immune from the drug and alcohol epidemic. Your child needs your strength and willingness to be involved with the fight against drugs and alcohol. It is never too early to start. Even before a child is born, parents can work on their attitudes that would be most supportive of a drug-free child. Likewise, it is never too late to intervene. If your child has already succumbed to the pressure to use, do not give up. There is a way to save your child. It requires tough love and perseverance. When you take action, there is hope. When you do nothing, you allow your child's future to be annihilated by the addiction bomb.

As a Christian parent, I urge you to take whatever measures you need to fight this problem with your kids, for your kids. Drugs will take the strongest faith in Christ and replace it with the power of instant relief and mood alteration. Nothing in our society has the power that drugs possess. They are cheap and available. You are your child's greatest hope for avoiding this plague of chemicals and elixirs. You, with the power of Christ, can win this war. But in order to win, you must be willing to fight. God bless you and your children as you do.

END NOTES

1. "Alcohol Use and Abuse in America," *The Gallup Report,* no. 265 (October 1987): p. 3.
2. Joseph Pereira, "Shunned Lessons—Even a School that Is a Leader in Drug War Grades Itself a Failure," *Wall Street Journal,* November 10, 1989, p. 1.
3. Stephen Arterburn and Jim Burns, *Drug-Proof Your Kids* (Pamona: Focus on the Family, 1989).

TWENTY-EIGHT

Five Great Things TV Can't Do for Your Children

V. Gilbert Beers

NOT LONG AGO THREE OF OUR GRANDCHILDREN stayed over-night with us. We like to do this from time to time to help us spend more quality time with each of them. But late in the day I felt the pressure to get some work done, too. My first instinct was to put a videotape in the VCR and plop the grandchildren in front of the tube.

You know the feeling, don't you? How many times this week have you turned to the TV as an electronic babysitter? How many times have you breathed a sigh of relief when the kids want to watch TV, thereby giving you some down time?

Sometimes that's okay, but too often we begin to lean heavily on the tube to babysit. Where is the boundary between enough and too much? I can't answer that question for you. You must judge for yourself and your family. But we both know there are dangerous boundaries where TV becomes a surrogate parent.

Consider some statistics. More homes in America (ninety-eight percent) have TV sets than indoor toilets. The typical middle-class American has at least three TV sets. The typical

American spends twenty-three hundred hours each year watching TV compared to two thousand hours each year earning a living (forty hours per week times fifty weeks). The average American child watches TV an average of six hours per day, as much time as he spends in school. By the time a child enters kindergarten, he has watched as much as eight thousand hours of TV.

To put it bluntly, TV-watching equals or exceeds bread-winning for adults and education for children. Put this in perspective with the time we spend in church, Sunday School, Christian activities, family devotions, or personal Bible study, and we easily become embarrassed. Who among us spends much more than four or five hours weekly on all these combined unless we are in career ministry?

Several years ago an important survey was conducted among evangelicals and fundamentalists to determine TV-watching habits. The survey concluded that the evangelical-fundamentalist population had essentialy the same TV-watching habits as society at large. If mom and dad are like everyone else in their TV habits, why should they complain if their children are like everyone else in their TV habits? With our children, our role-modeling will always win over our sermonizing.

So why should I care if my children watch TV the way their school friends do? Doesn't that free me to do my thing more?

First, consider those two thousand hours each year that your child "invests" in the tube. Is this the best use of two thousand hours? If your child spends that many hours with the tube, what's left for 1) family talk together, 2) family devotions, 3) good reading, 4) playtime, 5) creative develop-ment through good activities, and 6) quiet time, a time to grow without hype and glitz?

Second, are you *sure* you know what your child is watching? While the tube is babysitting, it is also indoc-trinating. It is teaching your child some severely distorted values. Almost everything you believe as a Christian is at times ridiculed and belittled or made to look unimportant on TV. Occasionally we see wholesome values emerge, but this has become the exception rather than the rule. We grow accustomed to the distorted idea that wrong is really okay after all.

Third, anytime you turn your parental task over to a group of high-powered strangers, you can expect them to do it their way. I really don't want a ratings-hungry producer raising my children or grandchildren.

Fourth, would you really want to raise your child by the lifestyle standards portrayed on the tube? Would you really want your child involved daily in real-life gore, violence, sex, coarse language, distorted family images, values vacuum, and anti-Christian thinking?

You and I would not think of exposing our children to all these things in real life. But we carelessly involve our children in a projection of these things into a bigger-than-life impact.

Fifth, contrast the pace on TV with the pace you desire in your family living. To paraphrase an old song title, "How do you keep them on the farm after they've watched TV?" What about our urgent needs, as children and adults, for quiet times, times to reflect or meditate about God, times to "smell the flowers," time to be creative, time to meet God? Your child cannot do any of these things while the tube is blasting at him full-tilt. Neither can you.

Sixth, are you satisfied with the typical TV character as a role model for your children? What if your child became this type of person? Would you be satisfied? Or do you have a different goal for your child?

It's easy to think that TV has so much hype and glitz that we parents can never compete with it: Our kids are hooked, so we may as well give up. That is a myth; it simply is not true. Your children are hungry for you as a person. TV can't even begin to compete with you if you are willing to personally involve yourself with your children and talk with them.

TV can't speak your child's name (or yours) unless generically by accident. TV has absolutely no personal interest in your child and does not even know that he exists. If he died, TV would not shed one tear. Your child is a nonperson, a mere statistic, nothing more than one more unit in the total audience profile. TV is totally disinterested in who your child is, what he thinks, how she acts, what he learned in school today, whether she loves God or hates him, and whether he loves you or hates you. Other than a marketing-profile statistic, TV has no personal concern for your child whatsoever.

But you, dear parent, have the opportunity—no, the privilege—of whispering your child's name to her a hundred times each day. And with it you can transmit vibes that no TV set can send out, vibes of personal concern and interest that your child is sure to pick up.

TV can't cuddle up with your child on its lap and read a book to him. TV has no lap, like my mother and father had, like Arlie and I have had, like you have, on which to hold the child. TV is not interested in flesh-and-blood contact, in touch, in personal warmth. There is no warm breath, no sound of a mother's heart beating, no twinkling eyes looking into my child's face, no sweet smile directed at that one VIP sitting on my lap, no one-on-one personal communications.

What TV said to your child this morning was not really said to your child. It was directed to a marketing image out there. Your child was included only as a statistic, not as a person with personal needs. What you said to your child this morning came from a heart of loving concern, a desire for that individual's success, a yearning for that one person to come to know God.

TV will never replace listening to a good book while sitting on a parent's lap unless we parents abdicate our royal rights and privileges and turn them over to strangers with a radically different agenda from ours.

TV will never hug your child when she cuts her finger or his friends make fun of him. At that moment of personal hurt and personal need, your child can never rush into his room, turn on the tube, and get the solace he needs. It's not there!

But *you* are there. It's your warm hug that counts at a time like that. All the five-star productions in New York are worthless at a moment like that. But a simple, yet loving, hug from mom or dad is everything.

Remember the power you possess in a hug. All the electronics in the world can never compete with a parent's loving hug, a tender embrace for a hurting little person. We adults need that too. We would gladly trade vast resources for a genuine hug from a caring person when life hits the fan.

TV will never replace a hug because it has no heart to care for your hurting child. Actually the tube has no brain to recognize your child's hurts. And it certainly has no arms to embrace him.

TV can never listen to your child. Among the many gifts a child wants from his parents is a listening ear. But TV has no ear. It cannot and will not listen when she rushes in the door and is excited about a new part in the school play. It cannot and will not listen when he wants to tell you about a new friend at school or getting on the Little League team. TV will ignore your child when she wants to ask the simple question "Do you still love me?"

TV reminds me of a storm sewer I watched following a thunderstorm. From somewhere the pipeline is filled and just keeps on flowing out, whether we like it or not. You can never send anything back through the pipeline; it's all one way. TV spills out its words and images, and if you're there, you get dumped on. But try asking it one simple question. Try telling it what's on your heart. It has no ears to hear, no heart to care if it could hear. You are a nobody, and your child is a nobody—just another statistical ear on which it can dump its one-way stream.

But you have a wonderful privilege when your child bursts through the door with exciting news: You can listen! At that moment you are more important to your child than all the TV sets in the world—if you truly listen! More than anything else at that moment, your child wants a listening ear with a direct connection to a caring heart.

TV can never replace a listening parent. It will never do that unless you relinquish your role as a listening parent! Then where else can your child turn but to the unsympathetic box with its steady barrage of uncaring words? And if we parents don't listen, how can we convince our child that God does?

TV can never tuck your child in bed at night and pray with him. Never! But you can. You have a one-in-a-million opportunity to do a simple act of love that all the TV producers in the world can't send out through those little boxes.

TV can't talk with your child about the good things and the not-so-good things that happened to her today. It will not put a soft hand on his brow and ask how he feels. It will not put a thermometer in her mouth and get a drink of water for her. It will not take hold of your child's hand gently and say, "I love you." TV will never kiss your child goodnight.

In case you don't know, you are the star of the show. TV can never compete with what you have to offer your child. You will far outshine TV in your child's eyes, unless you turn your parenting over to the tube.

Part 7

Looking Back

TWENTY-NINE

Relating to Adult Children Who Don't Share Your Beliefs

Joy Bolin

I T'S EASY TO SIT WITH A GROUP of young adults and share the truths of God's Word if you are in a Sunday School room conducting a Bible Class with a poster of "Jesus is Lord" behind you. No problem. But it's another matter when you are one-on-one with your adult child, eye-to-eye, heart-to-heart. Especially when that child, with each step of experience, seems to draw further and further away from the beliefs you tried to instill.

Some of us, who fully expected our children to carry on our religious expressions and basic beliefs, have been surprised. We forgot that freedom of choice allows change. So what happens when these adult children come to us and say that our way of life is great—for us, but not for them? Do we fly into a rage, turn our backs and walk away, or even worse, sulk in a lifetime of silence? I hope not.

Pain is inevitable when a child makes it clear he or she does not share your deeply-held beliefs about God, salvation, and living the faith. Unity is lost. Family gatherings, once eagerly anticipated, are now dreaded. How can the same family who laughed, cried, and played together, now be worlds apart? How are parents supposed to act—as if such differences don't matter? And yet, when does the demand for obedience end and a respect for independence begin? Scripture points out that God, in his benevolent love, gives freedom of choice to each of his children. When our children exercise their God-given freedom to turn away from God, should we go through life being alienated from them?

At a recent singles seminar, a young woman told me that even though she formerly enjoyed a close relationship with her mother, she now dreads every invitation from her. The mother is very generous, paying for the meal and choosing restaurants that specialize in her daughter's favorite food. However, no sooner do they get seated than the mother brings up their differences in spiritual habits, criticizing and pronouncing judgment on her daughter's chosen faith and practices. Nothing is ever resolved, just rehashed. The young woman now makes up excuses rather than face her Mom.

The mother was raised by strict, solemn, religious parents and adopted their persuasion. The daughter, an outgoing, stand-up-and-cheer type of person, has chosen a more expressive form of worship. The mother does not approve of her "emotionalism." By her repeated criticism, however, the mother is closing the door for any future sharing.

The meeting of the minds is a fragile exchange. If we really want to talk with our adult children about their beliefs, we've got to set the stage with comfort and erase all fear of rejection. Nothing is ever solved by cramming convictions down another's throat. But there are tried-and-true methods of keeping the door open for down-to-earth, honest, spiritual discussions.

TRY TO UNDERSTAND THE PAST

One that seldom fails, is a tough one: try to put on their shoes. Walk where they've walked. Try to identify the rugged canyons they've been in. If that tumble into despair had been ours, our torn bodies and spirits might be worse off than theirs. Somehow, somewhere, regardless of the straight, uncluttered path we tried to lay before them, they stumbled. Could it be that a big boulder of peer pressure kept them from seeing the detour sign? Or maybe permissive rules of society lured them in the wrong direction. When we place our feet in their prints, their rationale makes a lot more sense.

The story that follows is not an uncommon one. We've heard it before. Though the story is familiar, the ending might not be.

"I felt called to be a mother as surely as one who is called to the mission field. And I answered with the same excitement and enthusiasm!" the pretty Mom shared. She not only took pride in the two sons she bore, but truly enjoyed the tasks of motherhood. While her friends complained about all the washing, hours spent on soccer fields and in dentists' offices, she never resented any of it. God had called her to a special task, and she was happy doing it! We can well imagine her disbelief and firm denial when she realized that both boys had become addicts of drug and alcohol.

"How could I fail so miserably?" cried the mother. Both she and her husband had come from stable, happy, Christian homes and had established theirs in the same manner, with nightly prayers, Bible readings, and family discussions. Now, everything was completely out of focus.

As parents, they tried persuasion. Then yelling and lashing out with threats of, "How could you do this to me?" and "I never want to see you again!" The testimony of the mother continued, "Nothing could have prepared us for what we went through."

The younger son, whose habits began in his early teens, carried them over into college. The eldest began to see the futility of his life a few years after graduation. The years that followed were turbulent.

The mother shared with us how loudly the Apostle Paul's reminder of our duty to "pray without ceasing" shouted to her! "I couldn't do anything else!" she said. "I prayed from morning till night, and then I prayed *during* the night. I prayed in the car, in the shower, and over the laundry. I even prayed while I bathed the dog! I didn't think there was another mother on earth who knew what a broken heart was compared to the shattered condition of mine."

She asked her husband a million times what they had done wrong. She relived every day of the boys' lives and truly doubted that they would ever be a family again. It was during this time of questions and doubt that she realized something very important—God gives directions for the future, not explanations for the past. Then and only then did she understand what their position as parents should be. To heal the suffering of their hearts, they would have to reopen the door of communication with their sons.

Through counseling, they discovered the first step would have to be their willingness to forgive and ask forgiveness. Could they forgive the boys for the years of disappointment and hurt? Could the boys forgive them for their childish actions?

The parents took this step, and over time change has occurred. They would all agree that it has not been easy. However, the closeness is returning. The parents have developed a new respect for their grown sons. As the boys establish homes of their own, the basic teachings of their parents are remembered. The boys have many bad experiences to overcome; the gutters were too deep, the bottles too full, and the needles too sharp. But the comforting smiles, warm embraces, and open discussions are developing into a natural rapport. Once again they are able to share about differences of opinions and beliefs, resulting in acceptance of each other.

Unlike the mother who will not accept her daughter's change in worship habits, these parents have chosen not only to accept their sons, *as they are,* but are participating in their spiritual rebuilding. A combined effort of prayer, education, and willingness is the reason for their familial renewal.

TRY TO HEAR THE UNSPOKEN

Another way to succeed in keeping communication open on spiritual matters is to be willing to listen to your children's views. *Really* listen. This is not the time to sit with furrowed brows, preparing your spiritual rebuttal. It *is* the time to be a sounding board as your children sort through differences between their beliefs and desires and those they were raised with.

If there has ever been a time in history when exposure to all types of belief and practice was available, it is now. Free-spirited charismatics meet practitioners of solitude and spiritual disciplines. Those who've lived their whole lives in the church meet those who've never been inside a church. It happens daily. They sit together in the classroom, serve on the same boards, and live next door. Is it any wonder that our children are discovering new ways to approach their religion?

One wonderful Dad told us how surprised he was when his son announced his intention to raise his family under the umbrella of a denomination totally unlike theirs. The father admitted that he and his wife were not only disturbed and hurt, but even felt betrayed.

The son, who had married his college sweetheart, had

always been very involved in church activities, and had established sound spiritual habits at an early age. His wife came from a culture known for its color and pageantry and ancient doctrine. The parents had developed a good, loving relationship with their daughter-in-law. They found the uniqueness of the couple fascinating and enjoyable. Their only concern was the religious difference of their interfaith marriage. The denomination mentioned was a far cry from what either had been used to. Both parents questioned the decision and made known their disapproval. For the first time, a strained relationship developed among them.

Several months later, the son invited them to a special holiday celebration service. Reluctantly, they accepted. Admittedly, they were a little uncomfortable. But as their son and daughter-in-law participated in the order of worship, they became aware of the happiness and joy in their expressions. The father and mother were surprised to hear the truths shared about the holiday were the same as what they believed! "We were premature in judging the spiritual wisdom of our son. I can see why they were drawn to that congregation. The warmth and friendliness certainly met their needs."

How happy the parents were to realize their son had not left his early teaching at all, but, in fact, was carrying on with the same fervent devotion he had portrayed as a young boy.

We do not have to duplicate the spiritual posture of our children to maintain a close bond with them, any more than we have to eat the same breakfast cereal or drive the same automobile. Just as we taught them what foods were healthy, and what cars we felt gave the best performance, we taught them the importance of faith and worship. But if they are living by a different set of standards today, that doesn't necessarily mean they will be bound by those same rules five, ten, or twenty years from now. Especially if they recognize that the incorporation of our beliefs and the consistency of our lifestyle is still producing happiness, faithfulness, and love.

TRY TO FORGIVE THE UNCONFESSED

Of course, there are extreme cases and they have to be dealt with. Few of us find ourselves in the position of having to pick up the pieces and start all over again with an adult child. I know of one mother who did.

Two weeks before her daughter was to be released from the state penitentiary, she sat on the outer side of the visitor's screen. Opposite from her was her daughter; silent, withdrawn, and indifferent. The raging anger and rebellion of a few years ago no longer showed. Instead, there was a look of resignation. He tired eyes showed no glimmer of hope or expectancy. Old before her time, the young woman had experienced all the sordidness life has to offer.

After the sudden death of her father, the ugly scenes and arguments began. Day by day, she became more resentful of her mother, and grew to despise everything she stood for—especially the faith that comforted her in the grieving months that followed.

As she drove home from the prison, the mother remembered the total feeling of abandonment years before as the words of, "I hate you! I hate you!" were flung at her. These words lingered during the years she didn't know where her child was. When she was informed of her whereabouts, she was also told of the serious trouble she was in.

"How do you go about putting the past behind you? Do you erase all memories or just the ones that caused disappointment and heartache?" The mother assured us she did not have answers for these and other questions. But through her troubled thoughts, these words kept creeping in, "Be ye kind one to another. . . ." Oh, she knew the verse by heart, "And be ye kind one to another, tenderhearted, forgiving one another, even as God for Christ's sake hath forgiven you" (Eph 4:32). Could these words, written centuries ago, now have a special meaning just for her? Somehow, she knew there could be a new beginning for her and her daughter. A trust would have to be established, and since she had not been influenced by hate and confinement, it would have to begin with her.

Over and over we are taught to be forgiving of one another. Does being a parent exclude us from this same command toward our children? We all know how much easier it is to apply this to others than it is to our own child, especially one who has humiliated and hurt us so deeply. But according to the definition of Christ's love, there are no exceptions!

In no way does this suggest that we must overlook and willfully accept the sinful actions of our children. But it does remind us that the consequences of their actions will come from their disobedience to God. And even as parents, *especially* as parents, we are to practice mercy, kindness, and longsuffering.

The mother had asked for an understanding acceptance of the daughter she had lost. Her desire was to focus on encouraging her to look to the future. She shared with her about how God had quieted her fears with the words from the Scriptures and how he kept reminding her that the rebuilding would be slow, but that a relationship between them could be reestablished.

The words *respect, forgiveness,* and *prayer* are the three keys that point us to healthy and hopeful relationships with our adult children who don't share our beliefs.

Since it is usually the parent who sets the tone for either a continuing relationship or a more calculated one, we must be the doorkeepers of communication. We don't have to betray *our* convictions to enjoy these adult children who were once the little ones we tucked into bed. But we *do* have to allow them to establish theirs.

THIRTY

Failure Isn't Fatal: When Parents Make Mistakes

Louis and Melissa McBurney

"YOU CAN'T DO ANYTHING RIGHT, STUPID!" Have you ever caught yourself saying something like that to your child in a moment of total exasperation? I know I have. But more likely, my frustration erupts with a terse, "Here, let me do that." The words aren't as cruel, but the message is the same. Later we know we shouldn't have done that to our child.

Even more often, our mistakes were what we didn't say or do rather than some destructive outburst. Not paying attention, not praising, not setting a high priority on our children's activities, not listening. Andrea used to say, in tears, "Dad, you never listen." Oh, that hurt, but not as much as my not listening hurt her and Bruce and Brent.

I suspect all parents go through some of the hurt and guilt of not doing it perfectly. Parenting has lots of pitfalls. There are more ways to fail than you ever imagined when you first became a parent. Facing up to the mistakes, yet not being overcome by them, is what Melissa and I now realize is an essential task in parenting.

WE'RE NOT IN IT ALONE

One of the comforting realities we've discovered is that we really aren't in this thing alone. We've had lots of help along the way—good and bad.

The truth is, our children have many other influences in their lives. It's not a cop-out to acknowledge that fact. I remember when I was about fifteen and beginning to be interested in becoming a man. Dirty jokes on the playground, spicy words I never heard at home, tales of adventures with beer and broads all sounded curiously enticing. They were the worldly stuff we didn't talk much about in our church youth group. In the middle of the era I had a new friend who epitomized all of those risks and a few more I won't mention. One day I brought him home after school. Somehow my Dad was there and met my hero. After the friend left, Daddy said, "Louis, I don't know your buddy, but I can tell you he's trouble. You'd better be careful how much time you spend with him."

On one level, I thought I was fifteen and too smart for my Dad to tell me who to run around with or anything else. On some deeper level I knew he was right. I didn't understand how he knew, but his words confirmed a discomfort I felt. I moved away from the friendship when it became apparent I wasn't having a positive influence in the relationship. Dad was right. That young man ended up convicted of a felony and spending time in prison. In this day of drug abuse, sexual promiscuity, and disdain for moral values, the stakes are higher and the consequences grave.

Not only are our kids surrounded by individuals who can have a negative influence, but they live in a culture gone haywire. You've read the statistics. By the time a boy or girl gets out of high school his or her exposure to violence, sex, and purely secular philosophy is overwhelming. For a child developing individual identity with the strong pressure for peer acceptance, that's part of the process. Those exposures have a powerful effect.

It would be comforting to feel that our loving care as parents could prevent the negative attraction of those other forces. I'm convinced it can't. It certainly helps, but when the child's psychological task is to become healthily independent from parents, our influence may not always win out.

Besides the temptations that surround us and our children, there is another crucial factor: individual choice. We're all faced with tasting the forbidden fruit. I've wondered many times why God gave men volition. Even worse, he put it right into two-year-olds and teenagers. It's hard enough to cope with that choice as mature adults, say, fifty-two-year-olds. But there they are, our children, saying "no" to us and doing it their own way.

I watched our children make some choices I wish they hadn't made. Well, that's not entirely true. More usually I didn't see them making those choices, but only heard about them later. Then the heartache sets in as the consequences are lived through. It's not much comfort to know that they knew what was right and ultimately regretted the decisions. The pain is about the same, as far as I can tell. It does help relieve the guilt to know that we had at least taught them right from wrong, even though they chose the wrong.

I'm sounding a lot like a doomsday prophet. That's how we've felt as parents from time to time. There is one other way in which we're not "in it alone." Thank God! He's there, too. I'd like Melissa to tell you her story.

MELISSA'S STORY

A few years ago I was feeling like a failure as a mother. It seemed there were so many ways I had blown it with my children. The whole weight of their mistakes was a burden on my heart. It was so easy to sink into guilt and blame.

At about my lowest point in that remorse and self-incrimination, we went to a seminary for a conference. I was to speak to the seminary wives, and they had suggested, of all things, the topic of parenting. God knew I needed a new perspective. I certainly wasn't in a very comfortable position to talk about how to mother.

While trying to decide what I should tell these very young mothers, the Lord began to show me how he had filled in the gaps along the way. When I focused on my mistakes of the past, he changed my focus onto what he had been doing to compensate and fill in for me. I wished I had realized that at the time. Maybe I could tell that to these mothers in the midst of their struggle. When a mother's own selfishness conflicts with the selfishness of the child, sparks fly quickly. We don't begin parenting at the point in our lives where we have arrived at perfection. God is still working on parents as well as children. It was a relief to me to realize that he did not expect me to be able to do it just right. That is what he is there for.

We learn about him as we parent. Even in my failures, the Lord was there filling in the gaps. He cares about my children more than I do, and he'll redeem them. That's always been his action in our lives. He promised never to leave us or forsake us. That realization flooded my spirit with his peace.

I'm still concerned about our sons and daughter, and I still recognize my mistakes as a parent, but I don't sink into despair anymore. I can trust the Lord with them. He is doing a great job.

IT'S NEVER TOO LATE

We've discovered, working with clergy couples, that it is never too late for changes to be effective. Sure, it would be nice if we had done everything just right while our children were little. It also would have been glorious if the couples we counsel had felt loved as children. We've discovered though, that even as adults they find real healing when hurts from their childhood are made right. That's how we know it's never too late for us to make things right with our children.

One of the most difficult experiences in my life was also one of the most beneficial. I confessed my own failures and asked forgiveness from our oldest child, Bruce. About ten or so years ago, I realized that part of my failure with Bruce had been in not being very affectionate with him. I also realized that he probably thought that meant something was wrong with him. I went to Bruce and confessed that, as a brand-new mother, I was afraid of him. If he cried I didn't know what I'd done wrong. If he didn't smile like I thought all babies did I thought he didn't like me. The more anxious I got he more tense he was.

So I confessed all that to Bruce and asked his forgiveness. I could see the relief and understanding come into his eyes. He had thought I'd rejected him because he wasn't good enough. He was glad to forgive me. We both felt relieved of a terrible load. Our relationship began to improve from that very moment.

It's also never too late to show love. Part of my problem with Bruce was my discomfort with affection. I grew up in a family of non-touchers. This discomfort with affection affected all of my children, not only Bruce. When they got to be school age I seemed to just quit holding them very often. They didn't climb into my lap for stories, so I didn't pursue them. After all, in my family you didn't need all that gushy stuff. When I recognized how that affected me and how I was passing it on, I decided to change. I began making a conscious, deliberate effort to be affectionate.

At first it was hard to tell who was most uncomfortable, me or the kids. Our hugs were like two fenceposts embracing. Nevertheless, I faithfully stationed myself by the door when they left for school in the morning and when they came home in the afternoon. Slowly but surely, the stiffness melted into eager warmth. We all needed the love. Louis had no trouble at all getting into the act, and is clamoring to get back into the act now, so I'll give the pen back to him.

FORGIVENESS: BETTER LATE THAN NEVER

Another area where it's never too late is that of forgiving. Conflict and hurt are inevitable in a family. Let me say that in a different way. Conflicts and hurts are inescapable in parenting. I think you can see my point. Since the failures will be made, it is essential to have an escape. One way of coping is to deny the hurt and bury the pain. That doesn't work very well. The feelings just keep popping back up. Another way to deal with conflict is to get even. We've seen lots of families where this was done. That becomes highly destructive of everyone.

A third way is the biblical principle of forgiveness. Admitting the hurt, confronting the other person, but choosing to let it go. It's like saying, "I was very hurt and angry about what happened, but I'm not going to hold it against you. When the thoughts come back into my head, I'm going to turn them off. I won't rehearse it again. You're forgiven."

Some folks carry unforgiveness for years. That only builds barriers to relationships and compounds the failures. Conflict is inevitable, but it doesn't have to destroy families.

It's also never too late to give your blessing. This biblical practice has lost its meaning over the years, but not its power. In the Hebrew tradition the father gave "a blessing" to his children. It was his special stamp of approval for the next generation. That sense of being set apart, of being special endowed each person with a vital gift. Knowing our own worth enables us to cope with life with confidence and inner strength. Having the "blessing" empowers us to face failure or success with peace. Not having the "blessing" curses us to feel that we're not all right, whether we succeed or fail.

Perhaps the greatest tragedy is that when a person doesn't receive the parental blessing, it can't be passed on to the next generation. That makes it doubly important for us to be aware of whether we've given a blessing to our offspring. If you haven't given that special message of love, you may need to ask for it from your parents or appropriate the blessing given by God. He has the power to bestow it on his spiritual children. Then you can pass it on for the health and well-being of all your family. It's really never too late.

LOOKING FROM GOD'S PERSPECTIVE

It's a little bit insane, isn't it—suggesting we see something from God's perspective? As long as we're inhabiting our humanity, I suppose we'll be stuck in our human point of view. As the Apostle Paul said, "We see through a glass darkly." There may be two areas of life where this is particularly true. One is how we look at ourselves. The second is how we see others. As parents, our own failures and those of our children appear to be brilliant mistakes. There they stand, spotlighted before the world, heralded in blazing neon: history's most glaring error. I've imagined I was the star of the football follies, fumbling my way through fatherhood. As a psychiatrist I reward myself by imagining what my children might say about me to their psychiatrist! From that peculiar perspective, you can imagine how my mistakes must look.

It's comforting to be reminded that God's perspective is not the same. He said about David, the adulterer and murderer, "he's a man after my own heart." David's penitent spirit and life of faith in God seemed to blind God to his astounding failures. It didn't take away the consequences, but did make a difference in his acceptance to the Holy One of Israel. I'd like to believe that God's perception of my errors in parenting will come under the same nearsightedness. That his focus will be so much on my atonement that my mistakes are blurry in his sight.

One of the ways God's perception must be different has to do with priority. What's dreadfully important to me may not enter into his reckoning very much at all. For instance, where my children are concerned, personal comfort and achievement are always on my mind. I'd like Brent to be president of the United States someday if that's what he wants. He's been proclaiming that since he was four years old. It seems important to him, and therefore to me. Besides, being the first father wouldn't be bad. After some directional confusion, Andrea is finishing her degree in architecture and would enjoy some success in that area. I'd be ecstatically pleased to attend the ribbon-cutting ceremony for some structure she designs. They might even mention that her ability to perceive spacial relationships came from her father. Bruce and his wife Carolyn are in theatre. It's already been a thrill to see some of their dramatic work. I must admit that I'm out there in the footlights at every curtain call, vicariously enjoying the applause.

Yet, God may care little for their political position, vocational success, or public acclaim. His priority may preempt all of that. "Failure" in those areas so important to them and affirming to us as parents may be necessary from God's point of view. Necessary to bring each of them into a closer relationship with him. Can my need to be seen as a "good father" stand aside, accept failure, and let the priorities of our "perfect Father" work out a higher agenda? That's hard from a human point of view.

I've never totally settled for myself the whole question of

God's sovereignty. One thing I am sure about. Whether he causes everything to happen or allows some things or has taken his hands off altogether I don't know. I am convinced that he's busy bringing good out of bad and success out of failure. I function best when I can recognize his redemption of my failures. Especially in parenting that brings me hope. The things I did all wrong may create the platform from which God will work salvation for my children.

If that's going to happen I hope it won't take long!

Another aspect of my humanity is that my time is Bulova. Try as I might I'm locked into Mountain Standard Time's twenty-four hour days, seven days a week. I know God's clock is different, but a thousand years to me seems a whole lot like fifty-two thousand weeks.

I want God to work out whatever he's going to work out pretty soon. At times, parenting failures seem magnified by time rather than fading with every passing day.

Recently I counseled with a man who had suffered severe emotional trauma during childhood. He was a minister's son, but saw little of the love his father preached. He rebelled in every way he could and lived in anger and bitterness until after his father's death. Out of his grief and depression following the burial came new life. He began to understand himself and subsequently his father. In God's time he became a different person. His whole life was a blessing to others.

Now, in God's eternal time perspective, that was all wonderful. I suspect for my client's father the timing was lousy. He lived only to see the anger and rebellion. He lived every day with his own guilt and remorse. If he'd just been able to slip into God's vantage point, his distress may have eased. In fact the whole process might have been facilitated if the pressure generated by his sense of failure hadn't been focused on the rebellious son. Since we don't usually see things from God's perspective, I suppose we'll never know.

One thing I do know is that it doesn't help much for us to become locked into despair over our failures as parents. Melissa and I are thankful to God that, in spite of our goofs, we're not in it alone, it's never too late for change, and God sees it all in his eternal dimension.

Copyright Acknowledgments

Other Books on Marriage and Family Life from Servant Publications

Husbands, Wives, Parents, Children
Ralph Martin

A Christian family needs a lot more than communication techniques or discipline tips to flourish in today's society. Ralph Martin offers more. He describes a whole way of life rooted in Christian principles, then shows how to live that life in a non-Christian world. This book can help any couple strengthen their marriage and family. Martin examines all aspects of a husband and wife's relationship with each other and with their children—from sexual love to authority in the home. *$7.95*

10 Weeks to a Better Marriage
Randall and Therese Cirner

Marriages can always get better. You and your spouse can grow closer; your commitment to each other can be stronger; and your life together can be richer. In *Ten Weeks to a Better Marriage*, Randall and Therese Cirner show you how to improve the most intimate of all human relationships. Their 10-week program is scriptural, active, practical, well-organized, systematic, and just plain fun. The best news about *Ten Weeks to a Better Marriage* is that it is based on the good news. The program works because it shows you how to seek God's plan for marriage as revealed in Scripture and how to open yourself to the power of the Holy Spirit. Why wait? *$8.95*

The Obedient Child
Ken Wilson

A practical guide for training young children in confidence, character, and love of God. Ken Wilson lays down key principles and shares "hands-on" experience in showing how a biblically-based approach to training young children has produced positive results in his own family and many he has counseled. *$6.95*